VISION AND REVISION

IN YEATS'S *LAST POEMS*

Two Chinamen, behind them a third,
Are carved in lapis lazuli,
Over them flies a long-legged bird,
A symbol of longevity;
The third, doubtless a serving-man,
Carries a musical instrument.

JON STALLWORTHY

....

VISION AND REVISION

IN YEATS'S *LAST POEMS*

OXFORD

AT THE CLARENDON PRESS

1969

Oxford University Press, Ely House, London W. 1

GLASGOW   NEW YORK   TORONTO   MELBOURNE   WELLINGTON
CAPE TOWN   SALISBURY   IBADAN   NAIROBI   LUŞAKA   ADDIS ABABA
BOMBAY   CALCUTTA   MADRAS   KARACHI   LAHORE   DACCA
KUALA LUMPUR   SINGAPORE   HONG KONG   TOKYO

PRINTED IN GREAT BRITAIN

PREFACE

F OUR of the six essays in this book explore certain of Yeats's *Last Poems* through a reconstruction of their growth from manuscript to print. To that extent this is a sequel to my earlier book,[1] and since that included a general Introduction about the poet at work I have omitted such a discussion here. I consider no more than thirteen of the fifty-four poems in *Last Poems and Plays*,[2] because the drafts of several have been discussed elsewhere,[3] and because the drafts of many others reveal no significant development. Nor can my essays on the visionary aspects of the poems of Yeats's last two years claim to be comprehensive. To have attempted a complete survey in any detail would have involved much recapitulation of the work of other critics and would have resulted, I believe, in a book of small value and colossal proportions. I have, instead, confined myself to those visions and revisions that seemed to me important and were not discussed elsewhere.

Since Yeats's manuscripts and typescripts play a prominent part in my examination of the poems, a word must be said about my system of transcription. I use the abbreviations F. *r* and F. *v* throughout to distinguish between *recto* and *verso* (front and back) of a *folio*, or sheet of paper. Ff. = folios. While verse quotations from a printed source appear in roman type, single spaced, all transcriptions from manuscript are in double-spaced italic, and all transcriptions from typescript in double-spaced roman. This

[1] *Between the Lines/W. B. Yeats's Poetry in the Making*, second impression with corrections, 1965.

[2] 'Why Should Not Old Men Be Mad?', 'The Statesman's Holiday', and 'Crazy Jane on the Mountain' appeared in *On the Boiler*, 1939, but were omitted from Yeats's draft list of contents for *Last Poems and Two Plays*, 1939. They were restored, without his authority, to the rearranged *Last Poems and Plays*, 1940.

[3] Two in Curtis Bradford, *Yeats at Work*, 1965: 'The Gyres' and 'The Circus Animals' Desertion'; and three in *Between the Lines*: 'An Acre of Grass', 'A Bronze Head', and 'The Black Tower'.

enables corrections to be shown which Yeats, almost without exception, wrote *over* the line corrected. Thus, where in my transcription two lines are divided by a single space only, the upper and inset line is a correction of the lower. Yeats employed various forms of cancellation, all of which I represent by a straight line through the cancelled word or words, except where a passage is crossed out by a diagonal line or lines. In such cases I simply state that the passage is so crossed out. A dot enclosed by round brackets indicates a word that I cannot read; two dots, two words, and so on. Where an illegible word is crossed out it will appear in my transcription as (.). There can be no confusion with brackets in the poet's own punctuation, because he 'disliked a dash and detested brackets'.[1] When, in discussing a poem, I refer to a line number, my numbering is that of the final text as given in the *Variorum*: this I set out, for easy reference, at the start of the essay.

Of those many friends who have helped me with advice and criticism I am especially indebted to Professor Francis John Byrne, Dr. Oliver Edwards, Dame Helen Gardner, Dr. T. R. Henn, and Mr. Alf Mac Lochlainn. I should also like to thank the editors of *The Critical Quarterly*, *A Review of English Literature*, and *The Review of English Studies*, in which the first and the last two essays were published. The argument of the second essay appeared, in skeletal form, as part of my Introduction to *Yeats: Last Poems* (Casebook Series, Macmillan 1968). Senator Michael Yeats and Mrs. W. B. Yeats kindly gave me permission to publish the manuscript and typescript material in this book, all of which is copyright and may not be reproduced without written permission from Mrs. Yeats or from her heirs and executors.

J. S.

London 1967

---

[1] P. Allt, 'Yeats and the Revision of His Early Verse', *Hermathena*, nos. 63–6, p. 97.

CONTENTS

LIST OF ILLUSTRATIONS

I

THE DYNASTIC THEME

••

I

WHEN Beowulf first set foot, with his fourteen companions, on
Danish soil and was challenged by the Scylding coastguard, he

> Replied, opening the treasury of words:
> 'Men of the people of the Geats are we
> And household followers of Hygelac.
> My father was renowned among the nations,
> A noble chieftain, Ecgtheow by name;
> He lived for many winters, ere he passed,
> An old man, from his dwelling; every sage
> Throughout the world remembers him full well.
> With friendly purpose do we come to seek
> Thy master, the protector of his people,
> Healfdene's son.[1]

The son of Ecgtheow comes in search of Healfdene's son: for man
was defined by his lineage in the heroic age where the chief bonds of
society were loyalty to one's lord and duty to one's kin. This loyalty
and this duty, of course, traditionally extended not only through all
the affairs of life, but after life as well. The graves of ancestors were
revered, and in early medieval England when a man was killed

it was the duty of his kindred to take vengeance on the slayer or his
kindred, or to exact compensation. The fear of the action of the kindred
was originally the main force for the maintenance of order, and to the end
Anglo-Saxon law regarded homicide as the affair of the kindred, who
were entitled to receive the 'wergild', i.e. 'man-price', for any of their
members slain. Vengeance was no mere satisfaction of personal feeling,
but a duty that had to be carried out even when it ran counter to personal
inclination . . .[2]

[1] Mary E. Waterhouse (transl.), *Beowulf/in Modern English*, 1949, lines 259–69.
[2] Dorothy Whitelock, *The Beginnings of English Society*, 1952, p. 39.

A concern with the ties of blood—what I shall call the dynastic theme—is to be found in one form or another in most 'heroic' literatures, and in few more than in old Irish, or Scots, literature. The Irish early in their history, overflowing out of Ireland, occupied the western counties of Scotland and it was there that originated the songs and stories later attributed to the poet Ossian. These came to prominence in the mid-eighteenth century when James Macpherson, who at college between the ages of seventeen and twenty-two is said to have composed over four thousand verses, published his alleged translations, of which the best known are *Fingal* (in six books, 1761) and *Temora* (in eight books, 1763). One quotation (from 'The Death of Cuthullin') will be sufficient to give an idea of the character of his 'translation'.

'And is the son of Semo fallen?' said Carril with a sigh. 'Mournful are Tura's walls. Sorrow dwells at Dunscaï. Thy spouse is left alone in her youth. The son of thy love is alone! He shall come to Brogéla, and ask her why she weeps? He shall lift his eyes to the wall, and see his father's sword.

The controversy over the authenticity of Macpherson's Ossian poems contributed to the rising interest in early Irish history and literature. Many ancient manuscripts were edited and translated by such scholars as Eugene O'Curry (1796–1862) and John O'Donovan (1809–61), whose 'father ... on his death-bed repeated several times to his sons who were present his descent, and desired his eldest son, Michael, always to remember it' (*D.N.B.*). The Ossianic Society was 'founded on St. Patrick's Day, 1853, for the Preservation and Publication of MSS. in the Irish Language, illustrative of the Fenian period of Irish History, etc., with Literal Translations and Notes'. Sir Samuel Ferguson (1810–86) gave fresh impetus to what had been, until the middle of the nineteenth century, a largely academic movement with his popular *Lays of the Western Gael and Other Poems* (1865). The first poem in this book, 'The Tain-Quest', opens:

'Bear the cup to Sanchan Torpest; yield the bard his poet's meed;
What we've heard was but a foretaste; lays more lofty now succeed.
Though my stores be emptied well-nigh, twin bright cups there yet
    remain,—
Win them with the Raid of Cuailgne; chaunt us, Bard, the famous
    Tain!'

Thus, in hall of Gort, spake Guary; for the king, let truth be told,
Bounteous though he was, was weary giving goblets, giving gold, . . .

Yeats, whose play *The King's Threshold* was to have the same
chief characters and the same setting, would not have been blind to
the appropriateness of his buying the Norman tower in Gort. This,
however, was many years after he had written

> *Know, that I would accounted be*
> *True brother of a company*
> *That sang, to sweeten Ireland's wrong,*
> *Ballad and story, rann and song; . . .*
>
> *Nor may I less be counted one*
> *With Davis, Mangan, Ferguson, . . .*

It is not surprising that a young poet with this ambition should himself attempt a heroic tale: and, true to form, 'The Wanderings of
Oisin' opens—after the preliminary dialogue between the pagan
poet and St. Patrick—with a roll-call of the heroes.

> Caoilte, and Conan, and Finn were there,
> When we followed a deer with our baying hounds,
> With Bran, Sceolan, and Lomair,
> And passing the Firbolgs' burial-mounds,
> Came to the cairn-heaped grassy hill
> Where passionate Maeve is stony-still;[1]

The living heroes are forever mindful of the mighty dead. So, when
they meet the beautiful Niamh and she asks them why they are
downcast, Finn replies

> 'We think on Oscar's pencilled urn,
> And on the heroes lying slain
> On Gabhra's raven-covered plain;
> But where are your noble kith and kin,
> And from what country do you ride?'

She introduces herself in the approved epic style, 'My father and
my mother are Aengus and Edain,' and Oisin is soon bewitched:
whereupon

> Caoilte, Conan, and Finn came near,
> And wept, and raised their lamenting hands, . . .

---

[1] These lines did not appear in the poem as first published in 1889: only the three hounds
were then named.

The names of the heroes and their hounds, recurring through the
poem like a refrain,[1] serve to remind Oisin (and the reader) of the
world he has left behind him. The warrior-poet's last words echo
his first:

> when life in my body has ceased,
> I will go to Caoilte, and Conan, and Bran, Sceolan, Lomair,
> And dwell in the house of the Fenians, be they in flames or at feast.

In his close examination of the sources of this poem, Russell K.
Alspach shows Yeats's chief addition to 'The Lay of Oisin on the
Land of Youth' to be the conception of a third island—the Island
of Forgetfulness—where Oisin encounters the ancient heroes, the
kings of the Red Branch, and his own Fenian ancestors and companions.[2]

Two heroic legends that were to exert an even more lasting
fascination on Yeats's imagination than that of Oisin, Finn, and
Óscar were those of Cuchulain and Deirdre. The dynastic theme
runs through both tales, especially the former: and 'Cuchulain's
Fight with the Sea' tells, like Arnold's 'Sohrab and Rustum', of a
warrior father's killing of the warrior son he did not know he had
until the death-blow was delivered. The poem that followed this in
The Rose, 'The Rose of the World', introduces another epic cycle:

> For those red lips, with all their mournful pride,
> Mournful that no new wonder may betide,
> Troy passed away in one high funeral gleam,
> And Usna's children died.

His search for a satisfactory metaphor, or basis for comparison,
for Maud Gonne, led Yeats to Troy and a tribal vendetta on an
even more heroic scale than that in which 'Usna's children died'.
Again and again he returns to the Helen symbol that alone is
complex enough to convey his conflicting awe, apprehension, and
devotion.

> A girl arose that had red mournful lips
> And seemed the greatness of the world in tears,
> Doomed like Odysseus and the labouring ships
> And proud as Priam murdered with his peers . . .

---

[1] Book I, line 125; Book III, lines 5, 84, 104, 114, 116, 195, and 224.
[2] 'Some Sources of Yeats's *The Wanderings of Oisin*', *P.M.L.A.*, lviii, pp. 849–66.

Of all Yeats's adaptations and explorations of the Trojan story probably the most powerful is 'Leda and the Swan', where an entire dynastic theme is telescoped into one of the most brilliant sentences he ever wrote:

> A shudder in the loins engenders there
> The broken wall, the burning roof and tower
> And Agamemnon dead.

2

The poems collected in *In the Seven Woods* (1904) and *The Green Helmet and Other Poems* (1910) mark the main transitional period of Yeats's stylistic development, a transition that he himself summed up in 'A Coat'. The very title of his next collection, *Responsibilities* (1914), is indicative of the distance he has come since the days when he made his song a coat 'Covered with embroideries Out of old mythologies'. In the 'Introductory Rhymes' with which *Responsibilities* opens, Yeats addresses his *'old fathers'*: *'Old Dublin merchant'* . . . *'Old country scholar'* . . . *'Soldiers'* . . . *'Old merchant skipper'* . . . and *'You most of all, silent and fierce old man'*. He asks pardon of Jervis Yeats, the first of the Yeats line to live in Ireland; of his Butler and Armstrong ancestors; of his two great-grandfathers, Yeats and Middleton; and of his maternal grandfather, William Pollexfen:

> *Pardon that for a barren passion's sake,*
> *Although I have come close on forty-nine,*
> *I have no child, I have nothing but a book,*
> *Nothing but that to prove your blood and mine.*

The last line of the poem echoes lines 7 and 8:

> *Merchant and scholar who have left me blood*
> *That has not passed through any huxter's loin,*

and in that repetition of the key-word 'blood' is to be found, I suggest, a clue to the ancestry of Yeats's own dynastic theme here making its first appearance.[1] Blood is the chief currency of heroic literature: 'blood will have blood'; it is the supreme sacrifice a hero

---

[1] For a discussion of Yeats's genealogical investigations, undertaken with his sister Lily, see Joseph Ronsley, *Yeats's Autobiography*, 1968, pp. 12-13.

B

can make; the most prized possession he inherits from his father and in turn hands on to his son. The word runs like a dark thread through Yeats's poetry, the *Concordance* listing ninety-eight appearances (including twenty compound usages) in *The Variorum Edition of the Poems*.

Few works of art introduce a new subject, and few enough introduce a radical rehandling of an old subject: but the latter at least, I think can fairly be claimed for Yeats's 'Introductory Rhymes'. Whether the subjective application of a theme hitherto reserved for objective narrative can even qualify as a new theme is open to question. Prior to 1914 almost the only appearances of the dynastic theme in English poetry had been in narratives, chiefly epic, told in the third person. In addition, however, to the early heroic poems already discussed and such later members of the same family as 'Sohrab and Rustum', Tennyson's 'Ulysses', and Morris's versions of Scandinavian sagas,[1] there were a few more domestic tales like Wordsworth's 'Michael' or the 'Vaudracour and Juliette' episode from *The Prelude*. It is interesting to note that Wordsworth's great autobiographical poem contains only one brief reference to his mother, one to his father (though both, it is true, died when he was young), and none to his forefathers. His 'Ode on the Intimations of Immortality' starts from the premiss that 'The Child is father of the Man', but otherwise has only the most remote relation to the dynastic theme. Looking back, from a point in time when new books of verse containing poems about parents and children probably outnumber those that do not, to the work of the Victorian poets, the Romantics, the Augustans, the Metaphysicals, and the Elizabethans, one notices an almost total absence of such poems. The occasional exceptions— Patmore's 'Toys', Arnold's 'Rugby Chapel', Coleridge's 'Frost at Midnight', Cowper's 'On Receiving my Mother's Picture out of Norfolk', and Savage's 'The Bastard'—no more than prove the rule that the subject of blood-ties either did not interest poets or was not considered a poetic theme.

The events of the years 1916 and 1917 accelerated the flow of Yeats's creative energies. His imagination did not change course so

---

[1] For the influence of these on Yeats see Peter Faulkner, *William Morris and W. B. Yeats*, 1962.

much as cut deeper into its former channels. First of all there was the 1916 Easter Rising that seems to have taken him completely by surprise. His great elegy on the executed leaders, 'Easter 1916', is also a revealing self-commentary. The 'polite meaningless words' uttered against a background of 'grey Eighteenth-century houses' or 'Around the fire at the Club', the 'ignorant good-will', argument, and drunkenness of the leaders show how completely he was deceived by their 'casual comedy', how utterly they were transformed. Honour had returned to Ireland: she had found new heroes worthy of Cuchulain and the kings of the Red Branch. In 'Easter 1916', 'Sixteen Dead Men', and 'The Rose Tree' he repeats their names as in 'The Wanderings of Oisin' he had repeated the names of the Fenian heroes:

> I write it out in a verse—
> MacDonagh and MacBride
> And Connolly and Pearse . . .

An event of yet greater importance to the poet and his poetry was his marriage in 1917 to Georgie Hyde-Lees. Yeats was over fifty, 'the unmentionable odour of death' had for three years blown westward from Europe where a generation was being destroyed, and at home in Ireland a traditional, aristocratic way of life was on the wane. The last two of these factors he translated into characteristically personal terms in 'An Irish Airman Foresees his Death', 'In Memory of Major Robert Gregory', and 'Reprisals':

> Men that revere your father yet
> Are shot at on the open plain.
> Where may new-married women sit
> And suckle children now?

It is worth remembering that Mrs. Yeats was herself 'new-married' and expecting her first child on Gregory land when this poem was written. His own passionate attachment to Coole domain was almost equal to Lady Gregory's.

> A spot whereon the founders lived and died
> Seemed once more dear than life; ancestral trees,
> Or gardens rich in memory glorified
> Marriages, alliances and families,
> And every bride's ambition satisfied.

The decline and fall of a royal or noble house is a theme as old as tragedy, and there is little doubt that Yeats's poems about the Gregory household owe something of their resonance to his re-working of the Deirdre and Cuchulain stories and his *Sophocles' King Oedipus* 'A Version for the Modern Stage'. In 1918, with his own marriage only a few months old and the death of his 'dear friend's dear son' so recent, it is small wonder that he was increas-ingly preoccupied with the dynastic theme.

> God grant a blessing on this tower and cottage
> And on my heirs, if all remain unspoiled,

he wrote on taking possession of Thoor Ballylee, and in November of that year[1] addressed his wife in 'Under Saturn':

> how should I forget the wisdom that you brought,
> The comfort that you made? Although my wits have gone
> On a fantastic ride, my horse's flanks are spurred
> By childish memories of an old cross Pollexfen,
> And of a Middleton, whose name you never heard,
> And of a red-haired Yeats whose looks, although he died
> Before my time, seem like a vivid memory.
> You heard that labouring man who had served my people.
>   He said
> Upon the open road, near to the Sligo quay—
> No, no, not said, but cried it out—'You have come again,
> And surely after twenty years it was time to come.'
> I am thinking of a child's vow sworn in vain
> Never to leave that valley his fathers called their home.

This and the two previous quotations illustrate an essentially primi-tive concern with place, the 'paternal acres', that is frequently related to poetic handlings of the dynastic theme.

In February 1919 Yeats's daughter Anne was born and before she was a month old he was at work on 'A Prayer for my Daughter', which was not only to become one of his best and most popular poems, but also—as I attempt to show elsewhere[2]—one of his most influential. Its movement begins with the natural progression of a father's thoughts: will his daughter be beautiful? Better that she

---

[1] See Ellmann, *The Identity of Yeats*, second edition, 1964, p. 290. Yeats, however, dates it November 1919 in *Michael Robartes and the Dancer*, 1920.

[2] An extended version of this essay appeared in *The Critical Quarterly*, vii. 3 (1965), pp. 247–65.

should not be *too* beautiful: Helen's beauty, after all, brought her no happiness. At this point Yeats's meditation changes almost imperceptibly into reverse gear, as if the allusion to Helen of Troy in stanza IV had diverted him from the prayer for his daughter's future to a contemplation of Maud Gonne's past, that is at the same time his own. The two strands, precept and example, are beautifully woven together; the poet's voice rising through stanza VII to the bitter vehemence of stanza VIII, his harshness fading through stanza IX as his meditation again changes into forward gear. Maud Gonne, who might so easily have been his daughter's mother, is forgotten as the dynastically minded father concludes his prayer for the child's future:

> And may her bridegroom bring her to a house
> Where all's accustomed, ceremonious . . .

The 'Prayer for my Daughter' was followed in December 1921 by the less successful 'Prayer for my Son'. That year also saw the beginning of Yeats's 'Meditations in Time of Civil War' which, though they range far beyond the dynastic theme, start from his contemplation of 'My House', 'My Table', 'My Descendents'. In each section his imagination, with its unique ability to interrelate personal and public history, moves effortlessly between past, present, and future. The moorhen is seen to guide 'those feathered balls of soot' upon the stream, the honey-bees are bidden to 'Come build in the empty house of the stare'. In the animal kingdom as in man's domain succession is fundamental to the natural order.

Yeats's concern with dynastic continuity, which reaches its extreme in his advocacy of eugenic reform,[1] is inextricably related to his concern with the continuity of cultural tradition, especially in its more heroic manifestations. He sees the artist, maker of images, as custodian of this tradition and loses no opportunity to celebrate the artist as hero:

> My father upon the Abbey stage, before him a raging crowd:
> 'This land of Saints,' and then as the applause died out,
> 'Of plaster Saints'; his beautiful mischievous head thrown back.

It is his fellow artists that he celebrates in 'The Municipal Gallery

---

[1] See 'To-morrow's Revolution', *On the Boiler*, 1939, pp. 14–21.

Revisited', a poem commemorating the continuity of a cultural
tradition, that is followed by 'Are You Content?', a poem commemorating dynastic continuity. This, significantly, is given the
place of honour at the end of *New Poems* (1938). As in the 'Introductory Rhymes' to *Responsibilities*, Yeats again directly addresses
his ancestors. One by one he calls them up like the ghosts in 'All
Souls' Night'.

> I call on those that call me son,
> Grandson, or great-grandson,
> On uncles, aunts, great-uncles or great-aunts,
> To judge what I have done.
> Have I, that put it into words,
> Spoilt what old loins have sent?
> Eyes spiritualised by death can judge,
> I cannot, but I am not content.

Action is weighed against 'words' as in the earlier poem it was
against 'a book' and—in the manner of a prosecuting counsel—he
asks this jury to 'judge' (the word is used twice) whether he has
properly discharged his stewardship of the heritage transmitted
through their loins. Here, as elsewhere, the succession of family
names—Corbet, Pollexfen, Middleton, Butler—has an incantatory
effect similar to that of the roll-call of heroes in 'The Wanderings
of Oisin', 'Easter 1916', and 'The Rose Tree'. It is clear that Yeats
intended 'Are You Content?', with its recollection of

> He that in Sligo at Drumcliff
> Set up the old stone Cross,

to be followed by 'Under Ben Bulben', the opening poem of *Last
Poems and Two Plays*.[1] Nothing could be more in character than
that he should choose to be buried where he did, and to end his
valedictory poem with a celebration of the family connection with
that place:

> Under bare Ben Bulben's head
> In Drumcliff churchyard Yeats is laid.
> An ancestor was rector there
> Long years ago . . .

[1] See pp. 72-3.

3

Although, as I shall suggest later, the First World War was to have a profound long-term effect on the dynastic awareness of the participating nations, the English-speaking poets who were themselves caught up in it had at the time more urgent themes thrust upon them. The present was too much with them for there to be much thought of their forebears, and their personal future too remote—sometimes too improbable—for them to write many poems about sons or daughters. If, however, the dynastic theme did not find much subjective treatment in their poems of the war period, thoughts of the next generation were none the less lurking at the back of their minds. There is evidence of this in the work of the two best known of the English 'War Poets'. Rupert Brooke, one of whose last letters asked Dudley Ward to 'call a boy after me', wrote —with the bardic voice of 1914—in his sonnet 'The Dead':

> These laid the world away; poured out the red
> Sweet wine of youth; gave up the years to be
>   Of work and joy, and that unhoped serene,
>   That men call age; and those who would have been,
> Their sons, they gave, their immortality.

Wilfred Owen—with the very different voice of 1918—ends his bitter adaptation of the Old Testament story of Abraham and Isaac ('The Parable of the Old Man and The Young') with the angel

> Saying, Lay not thy hand upon the lad,
> Neither do anything to him. Behold,
> A ram, caught in a thicket by its horns;
> Offer the Ram of Pride instead of him.
> But the old man would not so, but slew his son,
> And half the seed of Europe, one by one.

Also relevant is the no less bitter conclusion of 'Dulce et Decorum Est':

> If you could hear, at every jolt, the blood
> Come gargling from the froth-corrupted lungs, . . .
> My friend, you would not tell with such high zest
> To children ardent for some desperate glory,
> The old Lie: Dulce et decorum est
> Pro patria mori.

Two years after the death of Brooke and one year before Owen's, there was born a poet who in 1968 is already more influential (at least among poets) than either. Robert Lowell, descended from a long line of New England brahmins including—on his mother's side—Edward Winslow, one of the Pilgrim Fathers, spent his childhood on Boston's exclusive Beacon Hill. Endowed with an ancestry, a tradition, and an environment that, one feels, would have had Yeats's whole-hearted approval (not to say envy), Lowell, who clearly learnt a good deal from Yeats, soon showed himself an unwilling inheritor. Hugh Staples, in his informative and perceptive study, *Robert Lowell/The First Twenty Years*, succinctly sums up Lowell's early attitudes:

> Dissatisfied with the Protestantism of his ancestors, he was not content to take up a merely agnostic position—instead he sought for spiritual values in the dogma of the Catholic Church. Finding Harvard, to which his family heritage had consigned him, something less than a nest of singing birds, he removed to Kenyon, where a new creative tradition was being developed by John Crowe Ransom. Unable to become, like his father, a naval officer, Lowell chose the role of conscientious objector, which he seems to have embraced with the zeal of a Christian martyr. In all these actions, he reveals a deep absorption in the historical sense without which, as T. S. Eliot pointed out in his famous essay, the individual talent cannot grow.

Lowell shows his 'deep absorption in the historical sense', as did Yeats before him, both in poems on historical subjects and in poems dealing with family history. At times the two historical frames of reference come together explicitly, and fuse, as in Yeats's roll-call of his ancestors:

> *A Butler or an Armstrong that withstood*
> *Beside the brackish waters of the Boyne*
> *James and his Irish when the Dutchman crossed;*

or Lowell's

> I envy the conspicuous
> waste of our grandparents on their grand tours—
> long-haired Victorian sages accepted the universe,
> while breezing on their trust funds through the world.

More often, however, there is an implied relationship between the two frames of reference; the one underlying the other. So Lowell,

writing explicitly of his father's failure and death in 'Commander
Lowell' and 'Terminal Days at Beverly Farms', writes implicitly of
the failure and death of a social class.

The central figure in Lowell's poems on the dynastic theme is,
however, not his father but his grandfather; just as the presence of
Yeats's maternal grandfather, William Pollexfen, overshadows that
of John Butler Yeats in the Irishman's poetry and prose. 'In
Memory of Arthur Winslow' is the central, and many would say the
finest, poem in Lowell's first volume, *Land of Unlikeness* (1944). The
first of its four parts is entitled 'Death from Cancer' and begins:

> This Easter, Arthur Winslow, less than dead,
> Your people set you up in Phillips' House
> To settle off your wrestling with the crab—
> The claws drop flesh upon your yachting blouse
> Until longshoreman Charon come and stab
> Through your adjusted bed
> And crush the crab.

This emphasis on his grandfather's cancer makes one feel that the
disease has a symbolic function in the poem: it is as if the terrible
physical rotting from within were in some way sign of a spiritual cancer resulting from the family's centuries of brutal materialism ('clip-
pers' and 'slavers') censured in parts three and four of the elegy.
Like so many of Lowell's poems, this opens with a specific locale:
Phillips' House, we learn from Staples, is the private, expensive divi-
sion of the Massachusetts General Hospital. The poet's continual
reference to recognizable topographical features of 'this planned
Babel of Boston where our money talks and multiplies the darkness
of a land', 'these hell-fire streets Of Boston', illustrates that concern
with the 'paternal acres' that is often associated with the dynastic
theme. Lowell shifts the scene in part two of the poem from his grandfather's death-bed to Dunbarton, the family cemetery: 'The stones
are yellow and the grass is gray Past Concord by the rotten lake'.
Yellow and gray, the colours of corruption, and 'the rotten lake' suggest an extension of the cancer that has brought Arthur Winslow to this

> hill
> Where crutch and trumpet meet the limousine
> And half-forgotten Starks and Winslows fill
> The granite plot . . .

The introduction of the family names reminds one of Yeats's Corbets and Pollexfens, just as the symbolic potency of Dunbarton in a sense parallels that of Drumcliff churchyard: although the very different views that the two poets hold of their ancestors conditions their view of their respective burial grounds.

From the burial service where 'The preacher's mouthings still Deafen my poor relations on the hill', Lowell turns in part three, 'Five Years Later', to a highly critical meditation on

> the craft
> That netted you a million dollars, late
> Hosing out gold in Colorado's waste,
> Then lost it all in Boston real estate.

Material prosperity is followed by poverty both material and spiritual: and in part four, 'A Prayer for my Grandfather to Our Lady', Lowell adapts and joins the story of the raising of Lazarus (John 11) and the parable of Dives and Lazarus (Luke 16).

> Beached
> On these dry flats of fishy real estate,
> O Mother, I implore
> Your scorched, blue thunderbreasts of love to pour
> Buckets of blessings on my burning head
> Until I rise like Lazarus from the dead:
> *Lavabis nos et super nivem delabor*

In his alteration of the *Miserere* Latin *me* to *nos* the poet makes it clear that his prayer is for himself as well as for his grandfather.

> 'Mother, run to the chalice, and bring back
> Blood on your finger-tips for Lazarus who was poor.'

Already in his first book we see the sequence of ideas that he was to explore further in his next three collections: the meditation on his forebears in which he struggles to understand them and, by understanding them, to understand himself.

'In Memory of Arthur Winslow' reappeared in Lowell's second book, *Lord Weary's Castle*, where it was supported by several other explorations of the dynastic theme. 'Mary Winslow' also opens with a death-bed scene: the Charles river now is frozen, but again it is identified with the Acheron and 'Charon, the Lubber' comes for the poet's grandmother as he came for his grandfather. The poem 'Rebellion' Staples describes as an

enigmatic nightmare-vision of patricide [that] is more than an expression of psychological hostility towards the father-figure as a symbol of authority; the identification of the father with the heirlooms makes it clear that the murder is a rejection of tradition as well:

> There was rebellion, father, when the mock
> French windows slammed and you hove backward, rammed
> Into your heirlooms, screens, a glass-cased clock,
> The highboy quaking to its toes.

The rebellion is not only against his father, but against his father's fathers:

> I dreamed the dead
> Caught at my knees and fell:
> And it was well
> With me, my father. Then
> Behemoth and Leviathan
> Devoured our mighty merchants.

In the long title-poem of Lowell's third collection to be published in America, *The Mills of the Kavanaughs*, Anne Kavanaugh meditates on the decay of the Kavanaugh fortune. Her husband, a suicide, had like Lowell's father been in the navy, and his signet ring bore the Winslow's motto: 'Cut down, we flourish.' It is, therefore, perhaps not too fanciful to suppose that Lowell is here carrying one stage further the patricide theme of 'Rebellion'. The naval father is not only dead, but childless: that his wife is the last of the Kavanaughs gives a grim irony to their motto. In what may be regarded at one level of interpretation as a wish-fulfilment fantasy, Lowell cuts down his family so that it shall no longer flourish. He stands in judgement on his ancestors and finds them guilty: quite the converse of Yeats, who humbly submits himself to judgement *by* his ancestors.

What would appear to be Lowell's final verdict, however, is not the death sentence. In Part Three of *Life Studies*, where he again and even more searchingly reviews his grandparents, parents, and himself when young, he begins to find positive values in the lives of his forebears and in the tradition they established, shaped, and he inherited. The affection and nostalgia for the presences of his child-hood that were not entirely suppressed in even the most guilt-tormented of his earlier poems now find their true level. Under-standing more he forgives more. The eleven titled poems of Part Three are so arranged as to make up one sequence, almost one poem. Each section, though complete in itself, derives strength and meaning from the others, especially the flanking sections. The first is entitled 'My Last Afternoon with Uncle Devereux Winslow', but is dominated by Arthur Winslow, as also are the two subse-quent sections, 'Dunbarton' and 'Grandparents'. Devereux Winslow 'was dying at twenty-nine' 'of the incurable Hodgkin's disease'; mention of which, like Arthur Winslow's cancer in Lowell's earlier elegy, seems to hint at some malignant spiritual disorder devouring the family from within. The first section ends with the five-and-a-half-year-old Lowell idly playing with

> piles
> of earth and lime,
> a black pile and a white pile . . .
> Come winter,
> Uncle Devereux would blend to the one colour.

And the second section coolly opens:

> When Uncle Devereux died,
> Daddy was still on sea-duty in the Pacific,
> it seemed spontaneous and proper
> for Mr. MacDonald, the farmer,
> Karl, the chauffeur, and even my Grandmother
> to say, 'your Father'. They meant my Grandfather.

Tender recollections of days in his grandparents' house are suc-ceeded by a section whose first line shows them to be dead. Then, in strict time sequence, follow the failure and death of his father, the selling of his 'cottage at Beverly Farms', and the death of his mother. 'Sailing Home from Rapallo' ends with a view of her coffin, and it is a most dramatic and moving transition to the child's crib that opens the next section, 'During Fever'.

So Yeats, having for years looked over his shoulder at the some-what oppressive shades of his ancestors, in 'A Prayer for my Daughter' looks forward into the future of his family. Although the greater part of 'During Fever' is a monologue addressed to his mother, and 'Waking in the Blue' is a reverie from 'the house for the "mentally ill" ', the last poem in this series returns to the subject of his daughter. She is addressed with charming and good-humoured tenderness: 'Dearest, I cannot loiter here / in lather like a polar bear'. My impression that these poems about his daughter mark Lowell's escape from the valley of the shadow of obsessive guilt, a return to health and hope, is reinforced by the poems in *For the Union Dead* (1964). These are calmer, more confident in tone, and the poet himself—as never before—is the protagonist. His ancestors have played their part and are banished to the wings. Although in 'Middle Age' he says:

> At every corner,
> I meet my Father,
> my age, still alive.

he writes now more as husband and father than son and grandson.

It is one thing to plot the development of the dynastic theme through the work of such other contemporary poets as Anne Sexton, Tony Connor, and Anthony Thwaite, but quite another matter to account for it. Though Yeats has been one of the most powerful poetic influences of this century, 'a siren whose rock is littered with the bones of lesser poets', one cannot attribute all post-1914 'dynastic' poems to imitation. There has, of course, been an element of this—sometimes a considerable element—but the main cause must lie deeper. One does not, after all, find poems about gyres and the phases of the moon in every second new volume of poetry that one picks up. Yeats himself, I believe, hinted at the main cause when he wrote of 'a child's vow sworn in vain Never to leave that valley his fathers called their home'. The structure of English society, and Irish society for that matter, changed less in the six centuries prior to the Industrial Revolution than in the century and a half that followed it. Until the end of the eighteenth century people in the main 'knew their place', literally and figuratively. Most of them lived where their families had lived for generations before them, as like as not at the same social level. With the progress of the Industrial Revolution this 'frozen' society began to thaw. The sons and grandsons of countrymen set off for the towns, on foot, on horseback, and then on the railways, and the distribution of wealth began to change. Through Victorian and Edwardian England the social thaw continued and the First World War further accelerated the processes of change. The battlefields of France took a proportionally heavier toll of the ruling class than the ruled, thus creating a vacuum that did not long remain unfilled.

Yeats then, with his concern for roots, was the first English-speaking poet to give expression to the rootlessness of modern man. Like a sailor establishing his position by the bisection of longitude and latitude, he looked to his ancestors and to his descendants to discover where he stood. If the First World War, as I suggested earlier, intensified the dynastic awareness of the English-speaking world, the Second World War—with its twin spectres of genocide and the atomic bomb—intensified it yet further. These, coupled with the decline of religious belief and the neuroses arising from the discoveries of Freud and Jung, would seem to account for man's present uncertainty as to his nature and his place. The confessional monologue from the psychiatrist's couch (of which an increasing number of writers have first-hand experience) has been adopted as a literary form: though some of its practitioners who subscribe to the view of 'poetry as therapy' would object to the phrase 'literary form' on the grounds that they have been trying to liberate literature from its forms, bringing it down to earth and back to life. The confessional monologue is, of course, no more an exclusively poetic phenomenon than the dynastic theme itself. Interesting parallels are to be seen in the development of the novel and the increasing popularity of biography and autobiography, but they lie beyond the scope of the present essay. Poetry and prose alike show today the influence of psychiatric method (*A la recherche du temps perdu*) for a psychiatric purpose (the attainment of self-knowledge). Frankness is all: many writers feel that the truth must be found and faced no matter what the cost.

So, paradoxically, at a time when the old morality is under assault from every side, when more is heard than ever before of the isolation of the individual, divorce and the breaking of families, we find the poets concerned—as never since the heroic age—with family relationships. Their message, it would seem, is Auden's: 'We must love one another or die.' It is perhaps not too fanciful to see a parallel between the society of *Beowulf* and our own: the one with its tribes banded against each other and the terrors of the dark unknown; the other rediscovering its dynastic sense under the threat of atomic war and the extinction of mankind. Consciously or subconsciously giving expression to man's innermost unrecognized hopes and fears, Yeats and the poets that have followed him prove themselves, in Ezra Pound's fine phrase, 'the antennae of the race'.

II

THE PROPHETIC VOICE

•••

I

'WHEN I was fifteen or sixteen', wrote Yeats in *The Trembling of the Veil*, 'my father had told me about Rossetti and Blake and given me their poetry to read.' This introduction to 'the voice of the Bard! Who Present, Past, & Future sees' was an event of considerable importance in the life and development of one who himself at that time aspired to be both poet and painter. Though it was not until the spring of 1889 that he began his close study of Blake's work, such of Yeats's early poems as 'The Indian upon God' (1886) show him to have been under Blake's influence some years before his collaboration with Edwin Ellis. Blake, it is clear, provided him with his first image of what a poet should be—an image that was to remain fundamentally unaltered for fifty years. The nature of that image and its hold on Yeats's imagination in his twenties and thirties is best reflected in the ardent prose of his essay 'William Blake and the Imagination' (1897):

There have been those who loved the future like a mistress, and the future mixed her breath into their breath and shook her hair about them, and hid them from the understanding of their times. William Blake was one of these men, and if he spoke confusedly and obscurely it was because he spoke of things for whose speaking he could find no models in the world he knew. He announced the religion of art. . . .

He had learned from Jacob Boehme and from old alchemist writers that imagination was the first emanation of divinity, 'the body of God,' 'the Divine members,' and he drew the deduction, which they did not draw, that the imaginative arts were therefore the greatest of Divine revelations. . . .[1]

[1] *Essays and Introductions*, 1961, pp. 111 and 112.

In another essay published in the same year Yeats speaks of Blake encouraging 'study of the works of great masters, who were great because they had been granted by divine favour a vision of the unfallen world from which others are kept apart. . .'.[1] Yeats, who had triumphantly announced to John O'Leary some years before that he had evidence that Blake was of Irish extraction,[2] in the essay just quoted again gives patriotism precedence over probability:

had he been a scholar of our time he would have . . . gone to Ireland and chosen for his symbols the sacred mountains, along whose sides the peasant still sees enchanted fires, and the divinities which have not faded from the belief . . . of simple hearts;

A man who 'loved the future', who 'announced the religion of art' declaring that 'the imaginative arts were . . . the greatest of Divine revelations', who—had he lived in the 1890s—would have 'chosen for his symbols the sacred mountains' of Ireland: Yeats's continual use of religious terminology shows the extent to which he regarded Blake as a prophet. Despite his new gospel, Blake seems cast in a curiously Old Testament prophetic mould. I would call particular attention to those 'sacred mountains'—presumably Ben Bulben and Knochnarea—on which the latter-day Blake is imagined seeking revelation. For obvious reasons prophets have been traditionally associated with high places since Moses descended from Sinai with the tables of the law. This tradition, significantly, Yeats was to adopt and adapt in the poetry of his later years.

If Blake was Yeats's first and most enduring literary influence, Shelley was his second. These two, he said, had shaped his life.[3] In his essay 'The Philosophy of Shelley's Poetry' (1900) he quotes with approval from *A Defence of Poetry*:

Poets, according to the circumstances of the age and nation in which they appeared, were called in the earliest epoch of the world legislators or prophets, and a poet essentially comprises and unites both these characters. For he not only beholds intensely the present as it is, and discovers those laws according to which present things are to be ordained, but he beholds the future in the present, and his thoughts are the germs of the flowers and the fruit of latest time.

---

[1] Ibid., 'William Blake and his Illustrations to the *Divine Comedy*', p. 117.
[2] A. Wade, ed., *The Letters of W. B. Yeats*, 1954, p. 125.
[3] *Essays and Introductions*, p. 424.

Of all Shelley's poetry Yeats predictably had the greatest admiration for *Prometheus Unbound*, parts of which his father read aloud to him when he was 'close upon seventeen': this—as much a 'prophetic book' as any by Blake—he counted 'among the sacred books of the world'. Its action, such as there is, takes place upon an 'eagle-baffling mountain', and it may well be that Yeats's poem 'The Man and the Echo' owes something to Shelley's 'many-voicéd echoes'.

In his essay on Shelley Yeats recounted how he had transposed *Prometheus Unbound* into an Irish key:

> I have re-read [it] for the first time for many years, in the woods of Drim-na-Rod, among the Echtge hills, and sometimes I have looked towards Slieve ná nOg where the country people say the last battle of the world shall be fought until the third day, when a priest shall lift a chalice, and a thousand years of peace begin.[1]

Among the Echtge hills Yeats perhaps recalled also Shelley's 'Lines Written among the Euganean Hills'. This poem, with the prophetic vision of ultimate freedom and love common to so many of Shelley's finest poems, was I believe one source—no doubt an unconscious source—of 'The Lake Isle of Innisfree'. The 'green isle'

> Where for me, and those I love,
> May a windless bower be built

surely anticipates the 'small cabin' on the 'lake isle', and it is hard to believe that the second stanza of Yeats's poem does not owe something to Shelley's

> Noon descends around me now:
> 'Tis the noon of autumn's glow,
> When a soft and purple mist . . .
> Fills the overflowing sky;

The way in which a prophetic vision of universal love is transmuted into an escapist dream of personal love is a significant measure of the distance between Yeats's poetry of the eighties and nineties and

[1] See also 'War', *Mythologies*, 1959, p. 110, and 'The Valley of the Black Pig', *Collected Poems*, 1950, p. 73.

that of the masters he wished to emulate, and was to emulate many years later.

In considering his debt to Shelley the prophet-poet, one cannot omit to mention *Hellas*, from which 'one passage above all', Yeats tells us in his *Autobiographies*, 'ran perpetually in my ears'.[1] He then quotes the thirty-five lines (by far the longest quotation in his book) beginning:

> Some feign that he is Enoch: others dream
> He was pre-Adamite, and has survived
> Cycles of generation and of ruin.

The old prophetic Jew Ahasuerus described in this passage captured Yeats's imagination, as Jeffares demonstrates in an article listing the many references to him in *Autobiographies*, letters, and even a review.[2] The relation of the great final chorus of *Hellas* to Yeats's 'Two Songs from a Play' is well known and a classic example of the way in which one poet's work can be absorbed by another and, subtly transmuted by the subconscious, pass from blood-stream to ink-flow as new poetry—in this case forty years later.

Shelley and Blake, though both religious in the widest sense, were united in their hatred of established religion, the Church and clergy, and it is clearly his masters' voices that one hears in Yeats's essay 'The Autumn of the Body' (1898): 'The arts are, I believe, about to take upon their shoulders the burdens that have fallen from the shoulders of the priests.' He foresees for the poets 'an ever more arduous search for an almost disembodied ecstasy'. This ecstasy, which is surely another name for 'that energy [Blake] called eternal delight'[3] and which Shelley associated with death,[4] is notably absent from the poems that Yeats was himself writing at this time. His prophecy, however, of the 'ever more arduous search for

---

[1] pp. 171–3.

[2] 'Yeats's "The Gyres": Sources and Symbolism', *Huntington Library Quarterly*, xv. 89–97. I do not accept Jeffares's identification of Ahasuerus with 'Old Rocky Face' of 'The Gyres', though Ahasuerus is, I am sure, a component element of that mysterious oracular figure. See p. 37.

[3] *Essays and Introductions*, p. 91.

[4] Ibid., pp. 71 and 72.
'The dying Lionel hears the song of the nightingale, and cries: . . .
> Heardst thou not, that those who die
> Awake in a world of ecstasy?'

an almost disembodied ecstasy' was certainly to be fulfilled in his own case, as his later poems testify. In 1901, when his early literary influences were being complemented and to some degree superseded by personal and political influences from the world around him, Yeats further developed his theme of the modern artist assuming the lapsed authority of the priest. His new faith is proclaimed in the title of his essay—'Ireland and the Arts'—and he takes the text, as well as the trappings, of his new religion from the old:

we must, I think, if we would win the people again, take upon ourselves the method and fervour of a priesthood. . . .
    The makers of religions have established their ceremonies, their form of art, upon fear of death, upon the hope of the father in his child, upon the love of man and woman. They have even gathered into their ceremonies the ceremonies of more ancient faiths. . . . They have re-named wells and images and given new meaning to ceremonies of spring and midsummer and harvest. In very early days the arts were so possessed by this method that they were almost inseparable from religion, going side by side with it into all life.[1]

As prophet of this new religion, or rather this rebirth of the oldest of religions, Yeats calls upon his countrymen to write of Ireland, rediscover its legends, celebrate its history. He no longer believes, as he did once (for like many of the most notable prophets he has experienced conversion), 'that art is tribeless, nationless, a blossom gathered in No Man's Land'.

    I would have our writers and craftsmen of many kinds master this history and these legends, and fix upon their memory the appearance of mountains and rivers and make it all visible again in their arts, so that Irishmen, even though they had gone thousands of miles away, would still be in their own country.[1]

To Shelley's symbolic mountains and rivers Yeats gave 'a local habitation and a name': but before considering the impact on Yeats of his discovery of a personal—through a national—identity, I must touch on the last and the least of the three major literary influences of his early years.

    In 'A General Introduction for my Work', written in 1937 for a complete edition which was never produced, he wrote: 'I owe my

[1] Ibid., pp. 203-4.

soul to Shakespeare, to Spenser and to Blake.'[1] It is clear that intellectually and temperamentally he had less in common with Spenser than with Shelley and Blake, and a Spenserian influence is most pronounced in such third-rate poems as the early 'Island of Statues' (1885) or the later 'Shepherd and Goatherd' (1918). In the Introduction to his edition of the *Poems of Spenser*, published in 1907, he shows himself to be more intelligently critical of Spenser than he was of his other early literary masters:

I have put into this book only those passages . . . that I want to remember. . . . I find that though I love symbolism, which is often the only fitting speech for some mystery of disembodied life, I am for the most part bored by allegory, which is made, as Blake says, 'by the daughters of memory,' and coldly, with no wizard frenzy.

Some pages later he had written:

Allegory and, to a much greater degree, symbolism are a natural language by which the soul when entranced, or even in ordinary sleep, communes with God and with angels.

In other words the allegorist and, 'to a much greater degree', the symbolist are prophets. Yeats saw Spenser primarily as 'a poet of the delighted senses', but knew that at his best he was more than this:

just as he was rising to something of Milton's grandeur in the fragment that has been called 'Mutabilitie,' 'the wandering companies that keep the woods,' as he called the Irish armies, drove him to his death.

'Mutabilitie' Yeats prints in full, and it is easy to see why he should have preferred this 'prophetic book' to the pastoral, pictorial rather than visionary, passages that he omitted from his selection. It is no great distance from Spenser's 'ever-whirling wheele Of Change, the which all mortall things doth sway,' to the Great Wheel of Giraldus and the twenty-eight phases of the moon.

2

Spenser's low opinion of the Irish is well known and he wrote scathingly of their 'Bardes and rythmers' who would sing the praises of anyone for

little reward, or a share of a stolne cow. . . . As of a most notorious thiefe

---

[1] Ibid., p. 519.

and wicked out-law, which had lived all his lifetime of spoyles and robberies, one of their Bardes in his praise will say, That he was none of the idle milke-sops that was brought up by the fire side, but that most of his dayes he spent in armes and valiant enterprises, that he did never eat his meat, before he had won it with his sword . . . .[1]

Yeats's own view of his forerunners, as reflected in his early stories and plays, was very different.[2] Before examining this, however, it is necessary to know something of the old Irish *bardi* and *fili*, whose traditions—so unlike those of Spenser, Shelley, and Blake—were influencing him at this time, largely as a result of his reading in John O'Leary's fine library of Irish books:[3]

according to the early metrical tracts the *bard* was simply a poet and versifier; the *fili* a poet, but also a scholar and guardian of traditional knowledge; he is especially a prophet and a seer and can wield supernatural powers. In short, he somewhat resembles in his functions the druid of pre-Christian Gaul.[4]

One wonders whether Yeats, as a boy setting off for England, was aware that the druids of Gaul were supposed to have studied their art in Britain; and that the candidate *fili*—whose formal training in language, prosody, and historical lore lasted twelve years—crossed the Irish sea to qualify in the art of divination. I think he must have had those 'singing schools' in mind when he wrote the second stanza of 'Sailing to Byzantium'. Though the office of *fili* is thought to have decayed during the Viking period, as late as 1651 Thomas Smyth, in his *Information for Ireland*, ends a brief description of the various categories of local poet: 'The fourth sort of Rymers is called fillis, which is to saye in English a poete. Theis men have great store of cattell and use all the trades of the others with an adicion of prophecies.'[5] Bearing in mind the *fili*'s line of descent from the ancient druids, it is not surprising that they came into early conflict with the Church. This conflict Yeats was to represent in 'The Wanderings of Oisin' by the confrontation between the Christian saint and

---

[1] E. C. Quiggin, 'Prolegomena to the Study of the Later Irish Bards 1200-1500', *Proceedings of the British Academy*, 1911-12, pp. 107-8.

[2] For a full and illuminating discussion of this important subject, see Constance De Kehoe, 'The Tradition of the Irish Poet in the Work of William Butler Yeats', Trinity College, Dublin, dissertation (unpublished).

[3] See W. B. Yeats, *Autobiographies*, 1955, p. 101.

[4] Eleanor Knott, *Irish Classical Poetry*, 1960, p. 7.   [5] Ibid., p. 9.

the pagan poet: he leaves us in no doubt as to where his own
sympathies lie.

In medieval Ireland the court poets were men of power and
station. Every feudal lord would have his family bard.

> His was an hereditary calling: *mac fileadh agus ua availi* '[to be] the son
> of a poet and the grandson of another poet' was one of the titles to the
> highest rank in the profession. He belonged to the aristocracy, to the
> *nemed*-grades, classes of privileged persons . . . .[1]

Certain bardic families can be traced for three hundred years or
more. They were the encyclopedias of their time, able to recite
historical, genealogical, heroic, encomiastic, satirical, and religious
poems. An early—and sure—indication of the power and influence
of the Irish poets was the energy expended by the English Govern-
ment in trying to put an end to them. An entry in the *Annals of the
Four Masters*, for example, records that 'Lord Furnival . . . harried a
large contingent of Ireland's poets, as: O'Daly of Meath, Hugh Oge
Magrath, Duffach son of the learned Eochaidh, and Maurice
O'Daly.'[2] As one might expect of the members of so ancient and
powerful a profession, arrogance appears to have been a dominant
characteristic. We have Murray O'Daly's ringing boast:

> This band in your house has come to you from afar. They were wont to
> quaff wine from the hand of kings or knights. . . .
> I am their master of teaching, many's the time I was in the midst of
> foreign counts; little ceremony I make, I sit in the presence of monarchs.[3]

One is reminded of *The Bounty of Sweden*, in which Yeats at the
Swedish court to receive his Nobel Prize was 'moved as if by some
religious ceremony'; and of his satisfaction at hearing that the
Swedish Royal Family 'liked him better than any previous Nobel
Prize winner', because he had the manners of a courtier.

At the other end of his life he wrote that, since he was a boy,
he had

> always longed to hear poems spoken to a harp, as I imagined Homer to
> have spoken his, for it is not natural to enjoy an art only when one is by one-
> self. . . . Images used to rise up before me . . . of wild-eyed men speaking

---

[1] Ibid., p. 55.
[2] See E. C. Quiggin, op. cit., for a useful discussion of this subject; also Myles Dillon,
Early Irish Literature, 1948, Chapter VIII.   [3] E. C. Quiggin, op. cit., p. 111.

harmoniously to murmuring wires while audiences in many-coloured robes listened, hushed and excited.[1]

In his fears for his failing eyesight Yeats was clearly a little comforted by the long tradition of blind but visionary poets. When he writes of Raftery, 'the greatest poet in Ireland', who immortalized the beauty of Mary Hynes, he quotes with evident approval the countryman who said:

'I think Raftery was altogether blind, but those that are blind have a way of seeing things, and have the power to know more, and to feel more, and to do more, and to guess more than those that have their sight, and a certain wit and a certain wisdom is given to them.'[2]

As Yeats himself put it thirty-three years later in 'The Tower':

> Strange, but the man who made the song was blind;
> Yet, now I have considered it, I find
> That nothing strange; the tragedy began
> With Homer that was a blind man,
> And Helen has all living hearts betrayed.

Homer and Helen, Raftery and Mary Hynes, Yeats and Maud Gonne—the sequence is implicit. He even provides one explicit signpost in the title of his essay: 'Dust hath closed Helen's Eye'. The year before this was published in *The Celtic Twilight* he had identified Maud Gonne with Helen in two of his best-known early poems, 'The Rose of the World' and 'The Sorrow of Love'.[3]

A number of other stories in *The Celtic Twilight* are concerned with poets and reveal something of Yeats's view at this time of the poet's time-honoured place in society; a view very different from the later one of the poet as outsider, outcast from society. If Raftery can be said to trace his descent from the exalted line of *fili*, 'The Last Gleeman' shows how far the bardic tradition had decayed by the early eighteenth century. Michael Moran, 'born about 1794 off Black Pitts, in the Liberties of Dublin', stands as *joglar* to Raftery's *troubadour*. He, too, 'went stone blind from illness', a fortnight after birth.

Once an officious peeler arrested him as a vagabond, but was triumphantly routed amid the laughter of the court, when Moran reminded

---

[1] 'Speaking to the Psaltery', *Essays and Introductions*, p. 14.   [2] *Mythologies*, pp. 28-9.
[3] Compare also the closing lines of 'An Enduring Heart', ibid., p. 36.

his worship of the precedent set by Homer, who was also, he declared, a poet, and a blind man, and a beggar man.[1]

Though, as I have said, Yeats did not subscribe to the view of the poet as social outcast, he entitled his story of Cumhal the gleeman (based on an eleventh-century Irish tale, *The Vision of Mac-Conglinne*) 'The Crucifixion of the Outcast'. In this the mysterious vagabond poet, whose 'abiding place was not upon the ridge of the earth', curses the inmates of an inhospitable Abbey in the language of Shelley and Blake: 'O cowardly and tyrannous race of monks, persecutors of the bard and the gleeman, haters of life and joy!' The abbot is informed, by a lay brother, that

'he is singing a bard's curse upon you, . . . and upon your father and your mother, and your grandfather and your grandmother, and upon all your relations.'
'Is he cursing in rhyme?'
'He is cursing in rhyme, and with two assonances in every line of his curse.'

The abbot recognizes the power of the pagan poet:

'Unless we do somewhat,' he said, 'he will teach his curses to the children in the street, and the girls spinning at the doors, and to the robbers upon Ben Bulben.'
'Shall I go, then,' said the other, 'and give him dry sods, a fresh loaf, clean water in a jug, clean foot-water, and a new blanket, . . .?'

This charitable suggestion from the (significantly) lay brother the abbot rejects. He has his own solution: 'we will crucify him'.

'The crosses are all full,' said the lay brother.
'Then we must make another cross. If we do not make an end of him another will, for who can eat and sleep in peace while men like him are going about the world?'

Accordingly, next morning the gleeman is crucified by the monks, and stoned by the beggars to whom he had given the last food from his wallet. The purpose of this savagely ironic Christ-allegory is to show the poet outcast not by society, but by the 'cowardly and tyrannous race of monks, . . . haters of life and joy'.

The most complete portrait of a poet in Yeats's early prose writings is that of Red Hanrahan, 'the learned man and the great

[1] Ibid., p. 50.

songmaker', who is modelled on the eighteenth-century peasant
poet Owen Roe [Red] O'Sullivan.

> And I myself created Hanrahan
> And drove him drunk or sober through the dawn . . .

Like Michael Gillane in *Cathleen Ni Houlihan*, Hanrahan forsakes
and forgets an earthly love for an unearthly woman, 'the most
beautiful the world ever saw', who appears to him in a vision on
'one of the slopes of Slieve Echtge'. His love songs are succeeded
by—or transformed into—'songs about Ireland and her griefs':

> The old brown thorn-trees break in two high over Cummen Strand,
> Under a bitter black wind that blows from the left hand;
> Our courage breaks like an old tree in a black wind and dies,
> For we have hidden in our hearts the flame out of the eyes
> Of Cathleen, the daughter of Houlihan.

Just as Hanrahan's creator was at this time trying to look beyond
Maud Gonne to Cathleen Ni Houlihan, Yeats's boast of 1918—
'And I may dine at journey's end With Landor and with Donne'—
is an echo of Hanrahan's: 'And it is with the rest of the poets I myself will be sitting and talking in some place far beyond the world
to the end of life and time.' After a second vision—of 'the Sidhe,
the ancient defeated gods' on the top of Ben Bulben—'it seemed as
if he was beginning to belong to some world out of sight and misty';
and when at last he dies, in a high cabin on a hillside, he hears
about him 'faint, joyful voices' and 'the continual clashing of
swords'.[1] Like Raftery on his deathbed, Hanrahan is engulfed in a
blinding light 'full of great shadowy figures'. The prophet-poet
enters his ultimate revelation on the mountain.

3

The bardic heroes of Yeats's early poems and plays are patently
romantic projections of himself:

> First that sea-rider Oisin led by the nose
> Through three enchanted islands, allegorical dreams,
> Vain gaiety, vain battle, vain repose,
> Themes of the embittered heart . . .

---

[1] Compare 'To Some I have Talked with by the Fire', line 13, and *At the Hawk's Well*,
lines 241 and 245.

Critics may differ on whether or not the 'three enchanted islands' represent Sligo, London, and Howth,[1] but most are agreed that, at one level of interpretation, Oisin's journey is an allegory of Yeats's own experience. The pagan poet reappears in *The Countess Cathleen* (1892) as Aleel the lute-player, whose high place in his mistress's household and affections is shown by her leaning on his arm rather than that of Oona her Christian foster-mother. The Countess recognizes Aleel's second sight:

> So it is true what I have heard men say,
> That you have seen and heard what others cannot.

It is the pagan poet rather than the Christian foster-mother who prophesies her death and, at the fulfilment of that prophecy, sees the vision of Hell—a pagan hell. Aleel, not Oona, sees 'Angels and devils clash in the middle air', and it is he who finally arrests the angel, forcing it to recount Cathleen's ascension into a Christian heaven.

Seanchan of *The King's Threshold* (1904),[2] Chief Poet of Ireland, was created less in his maker's image than Aleel the dreamy court poet. Yeats's resemblance to Seanchan was to grow as he grew older. It was appropriate that the creator of the poet who 'fasted unto death' in protest at being excluded from the council of the State should in 1922 himself be elected to the Irish Senate to sit among the 'Bishops, Soldiers, and Makers of the Law'. In his story 'The Wisdom of the King' Yeats depicts the High King of Ireland calling together his 'poets and men of law' to advise him; and when the king dies 'the poets and the men of law were called together by the chief poet'.[3] Seanchan dies to uphold 'the poets' right, Established at the establishment of the world'. By this act, it is implied, the temporal power of the monarchy will be overthrown by the supernatural power of the poets.[4]

Forgael, the harpist-hero of *The Shadowy Waters* (1911), is more

---

[1] Ellmann, *The Identity of Yeats*, second edition, 1964, p. 17.

[2] Seanchan Torpeist was a historical figure: see p. 2. Yeats, in a note to this play, wrote that he 'took the plot of it from a Middle Irish story about the demands of the poets at the court of King Guaire, but twisted it about and revised its moral that the poet might have the best of it'.   [3] *Mythologies*, p. 167.

[4] For a perceptive discussion of this play see S. B. Bushrui, '*The King's Threshold*: A Defence of Poetry', *A Review of English Literature*, iv. 3, pp. 81-94.

akin to Aleel than Seanchan. Dectora speaks of his 'Druid craft of
wicked music' and tells the sailors: 'He has flung a Druid spell upon
the air, And set you dreaming.' The music of his harp bewitches the
sailors and in a moment turns her thoughts from murder to love—
an effect that Yeats looked in vain for his own 'passionate rhyme'
to have on Maud Gonne. Sea birds are Forgael's pilots: they have
promised to bring him 'to unheard-of passion, To some strange love
the world knows nothing of, Some Ever-living woman'. Their
prophetic promise is fulfilled as is the prophecy made to Aleel by
the stranger in his dream who 'had birds about his head'. In making
birds symbolic emissaries between earth and sky, natural and supernatural, Yeats is of course building on ancient traditions of divination and the transmigration of souls.

In such of his later plays as *Deirdre*, *At the Hawk's Well*, and *The
Cat and the Moon*, the prophetic poet as hero is replaced by the
musicians as prophetic chorus, but the early poems like the early
plays are dominated by the presence of the Poet. He declares himself in his titles: 'A Poet to his Beloved', 'The Poet pleads with the
Elemental Powers'. The poems grouped under the heading 'Cross-
ways' in the 1895 *Poems* are dominated by 'sorrow', a word that
appears twenty-two times; it occurs fifteen times in the final version
of 'The Wanderings of Oisin'. Although this is hardly surprising in
view of Yeats's unhappiness at this period, the twilit melancholy of
these poems, with all their introspection and retrospection, makes
a sharp contrast with the vigorous poetry of his admired masters
Shelley and Blake. He was at this stage self-obsessed and his poetic
landscape, coloured by his grief, abounds in images of water—
lakes and seas—that have a feminine and even narcissistic quality.
Yeats, one feels, is a little like the parrot in 'The Indian to his Love'
that 'sways upon a tree, Raging at his own image in the enamelled
sea'. His eyes are generally downcast or looking over his shoulder.
He is in love with a past even further from his reach than Maud
Gonne herself:

> *I would, before my time to go,*
> *Sing of old Eire and the ancient ways:*
> *Red Rose, proud Rose, sad Rose of all my days.*

This, the first and title-poem of *The Rose*, is counterbalanced, it must be said, by 'To Ireland in the Coming Times', but that is not the forward-looking, prophetic poem its title suggests.

> While still I may, I write for you
> The love I lived, the dream I knew.

Those past tenses 'lived' and 'knew' betray a retrospective vision.

Though we see this vision extending in the poems of *In the Seven Woods* (1904), *The Green Helmet* (1910), and *Responsibilities* (1914) to include the present, Yeats is not yet able to focus at the same time on 'what is past, or passing, or to come'. There is a new note of resolution, however, in 'A Coat', the penultimate poem of *Responsibilities*:

> I made my song a coat
> Covered with embroideries
> Out of old mythologies
> From heel to throat.

In the slightly facile rhyme 'embroideries'/'mythologies' one seems to detect a note of impatience with the muffling coat he is casting off, and a sense of sharpened anticipation is introduced by the feminine half-rhyme of the last three lines:

> Song, let them take it,
> For there's more enterprise
> In walking naked.

This eight-line poem, I suggest, contains not only Yeats's old style and his new but, inseparable from these, his early backward vision and his later prophetic vision. So Lear, growing into self-knowledge and a terrible awareness of the world about him, cries: 'Off, off, you lendings! Come, unbutton here.'

At the start of his next collection of poems Yeats sees the nine-and-fifty swans on Coole lake

> All suddenly mount
> And scatter wheeling in great broken rings
> Upon their clamorous wings.

His eyes are lifted from lake to sky, where the white birds transfigure the October twilight. They are 'mysterious, beautiful', an echo no doubt unconscious (but significant in its magical connotations) of the 'arm Clothed in white samite, mystic, wonderful' that rises from 'the shining levels' of another lake to catch Excalibur in Tennyson's 'Morte d'Arthur'. The ageing Yeats sees the wild swans as unageing, and their confident energy communicates itself to his poem. As they 'climb the air', so in the following poem—'In Memory of Major Robert Gregory'—Yeats says:

> I'll name the friends that cannot sup with us
> Beside a fire of turf in th'ancient tower,
> And having talked to some late hour
> Climb up the narrow winding stair to bed:

Like a prophet to his mountain top, or a priest to his pulpit, Yeats for the next twenty years was to 'climb to the tower-top and lean upon broken stone'. The increasingly prophetic poems of these years abound in images of climbing—the Irish Airman, the Fisherman 'Climbing to a place Where stone is dark under froth'—and masculine rock replaces feminine water as the predominant element of his poetic landscape.

The seemingly deathless wild swans at Coole 'delight men's eyes'; Major Robert Gregory is driven by 'a lonely impulse of delight' to the fatal 'tumult in the clouds'; and Yeats, in his elegy on his 'dear friend's dear son', reflects that 'all things the delighted eye now sees Were loved by him'. Delight—a rare emotion in his early poetry—from 1917, the year of his marriage, takes the place of sorrow, a word that appears in only two poems written after 1900. Mrs. Yeats, it is clear, brought her husband his new delight, as he acknowledges in 'The Gift of Harun Al-Rashid', a poem whose drafts contain the cancelled lines: 'And that was my first news of her that now Is my delight & comfort'.[1] Literature owes more to Georgina Hyde-Lees, whose automatic writing provided Yeats with the framework for most of the finest poems of his last twenty years, than to Maud Gonne. The change from sorrow to delight seems the more remarkable when one considers the private griefs and public disappointments that beset him, and his growing awareness of death. Further light is shed on this apparent paradox by his poem 'Upon a Dying Lady'. Section VI of that elegy on Mabel Beardsley is entitled

---

[1] See Jon Stallworthy, *Between the Lines/W. B. Yeats's Poetry in the Making*, 1963, p. 78.

Her Courage, and in it the poet asks that her soul, after death, should

> come face to face
> Amid that first astonishment with Grania's shade, . . .
> Aye, and Achilles, Timor, Babar, Barhaim, all
> Who have lived in joy and laughed into the face of Death.

The more Yeats saw of death the more he became convinced that

> Whether man die in his bed
> Or the rifle knocks him dead,
> A brief parting from those dear
> Is the worst man has to fear.

Armed with this belief in an afterlife he came to the conviction that one must live in joy and—like the ancient heroes—laugh into the face of Death; 'come Proud, open-eyed and laughing to the tomb'.[1] He saw beyond his own terrible vision of 'The Second Coming'. Shelley's Ahasuerus was said to have 'survived Cycles of generation and of ruin', and Yeats was I am sure deliberate in following 'The Second Coming' with 'A Prayer for my Daughter', in which the storm symbolic of the coming fury is preceded and succeeded by images of generation.

In 1931 he met Shri Purohit, a swami visiting England, and for the last eight years of his life his attention was drawn back to the India that he had first seen through the eyes of Mohini Chatterjee in 1885. In his early dramatic poem 'Anashuya and Vijaya' Yeats's hero had asked his love to

> Swear by the parents of the gods,
> Dread oath, who dwell on sacred Himalay,
> On the far Golden Peak;

so it was appropriate that in 1934 he should introduce the swami's translation from the Marathi of *The Holy Mountain*. As with many of Yeats's Introductions this sheds as much light on himself and his concerns as on his avowed subject.

To Indians, Chinese, and Mongols, mountains from the earliest times have been the dwelling-places of the Gods. Their kings before any great

---

[1] For the influence of Nietzsche's concept of 'laughter' on Yeats, see S. B. Bushrui, op. cit., pp. 92–3.

decision have climbed some mountain, and of all these mountains Kailās, or Mount Meru, as it is called in the *Mahabharata*, was the most famous.[1]

He goes on to tell of the thousands of pilgrims that have encircled it 'measuring the ground with their bodies; an outer ring for all, an inner and more perilous for those called by the priests to its greater penance'. Yeats adds in commentary: 'We too have learnt from Dante to imagine our Eden, or Earthly Paradise, upon a mountain, penitential rings upon the slope.' His reading of *The Holy Mountain* gave him the material for his poem 'Meru', on which he provided a useful note:

I said [to an Irish poet during a country walk] that for the moment I associated early Christian Ireland with India; Shri Purohit Swami, pro-tected during his pilgrimage to a remote Himalayan shrine by a strange great dog that disappeared when danger was past, might have been that blessed Cellach who sang upon his deathbed of bird and beast; Bagwan Shri Hamsa's pilgrimage to Mount Kailás, the legendary Meru, and to lake Manas Sarowa, suggested pilgrimages to Croagh Patrick and to Lough Derg.[2]

The sonnet 'Meru', which presents the vision of 'Hermits upon Mount Meru or Everest', ends the sequence of 'Supernatural Songs', the first four of which record the vision of the Irish hermit Ribh. Yeats, through the eyes of the Oriental ascetic, sees that man

> despite his terror, cannot cease
> Ravening through century after century,
> Ravening, raging, and uprooting that he may come
> Into the desolation of reality:

One might consider this a conclusion of total despair, but for the strongly buoyant—even exultant—rhythm of the line that follows: 'Egypt and Greece, good-bye, and good-bye, Rome!'[3] There is a similar movement in the opening line of 'The Gyres': 'The gyres! the gyres! Old Rocky Face, look forth;' and one must wonder here at the skill with which Yeats links not only poem with poem, but book with book. Old Rocky Face—glossed in Mrs. Yeats's copy of

[1] *Essays and Introductions*, p. 455.

[2] *The Variorum Edition of the Poems*, 1957, p. 837.

[3] Compare *The Resurrection*, lines 401-2: 'O Athens, Alexandria, Rome, something has come to destroy you.'

the *Last Poems* as 'Delphic Oracle'[1]—is clearly a development of the
hermit upon Mount Meru 'Caverned in night'. In the drafts of 'The
Gyres' Old Rocky Face even appears as 'Old cavern man, old rocky
face'.[2] He is also described as 'wrinkled rocky face'[3]—an anticipation of the 'eyes mid many wrinkles' that look out 'On all the tragic
scene' from the carving of lapis lazuli. The comparison of Oriental
ascetic with Delphic oracle Yeats had already hinted at in his Introduction to *The Holy Mountain* when, towards the end, he quoted
the words of the chorus from his own translation of *Sophocles' King
Oedipus*:

> should a man forget
> The holy images, the Delphian Sibyl's trance,
> And the world's navel-stone, and not be punished for it
> And seem most fortunate, or even blessed perchance,
> Why should we honour the Gods, or join the sacred dance?

It is generally agreed that the Rocky Face of 'The Gyres', the Rocky
Voice of 'The Man and the Echo', is compounded of Delphic
oracle, Oriental ascetic, the cave-dwelling Ahasuerus, and an echo
or recollection of the phrase 'rockie face' in Ben Jonson's poem 'My
Picture Left in Scotland'.[4] T. R. Henn has called attention to what,
I am convinced, must have been a fifth element in its composition:
'the caved stone head, high in the S.E. wall of Thoor Ballylee'.[5]
Yeats would naturally have identified himself with the weathered
face staring out towards Coole Park, whose ruin he had correctly
prophesied in 'Coole Park, 1929'. Extending this line of thought,
it is tempting to speculate on whether he may not have had Robert
Gregory in mind when he wrote: 'Hector is dead and there's a light
in Troy.'

Old Rocky Face's vision of the gyres is clearly related to the
ascetic's view from Meru of 'Civilization . . . hooped together'. It
is the 'Ravening through century after century' that Old Rocky
Face sees at closer range as 'a light in Troy'. He can afford to 'laugh
in tragic joy', just as the ascetic could exclaim with something

---

[1] Curtis Bradford, *Yeats at Work*, 1965, p. 148.
[2] Ibid., p. 145.
[3] Ibid., p. 143.
[4] D. Donoghue and J. R. Mulryne, eds., *An Honoured Guest*, 1965, pp. 125–6.
[5] *The Lonely Tower*, second edition, 1965, p. 321.

D

approaching gaiety, 'Egypt and Greece, good-bye,' because he sees
the alternation of the 'Cycles of generation and of ruin', and knows
the one would be impossible without the other. The ascetic's
illumination comes upon him, in the time-honoured Neoplatonic
tradition, when he is 'Caverned in night'. So, in his Introduction to
The Holy Mountain Yeats quotes Vaughan:

> There is in God, some say
> A deep but dazzling darkness: . . .

Related to this concept is Yeats's belief that as day follows night the
new gyre rises from darkness:

> From marble of a broken sepulchre,
> Or dark betwixt the polecat and the owl,
> Or any rich, dark nothing disinter
> The workman, noble and saint, and all things run
> On that unfashionable gyre again.

Similarly, 'The Statues' ends with an assertion of magnificent
arrogance worthy of Yeats's bardic predecessors:

> We Irish, born into that ancient sect
> But thrown upon this filthy modern tide
> And by its formless spawning fury wrecked,
> Climb to our proper dark . . .

The poem that is perhaps the most eloquent statement of the
ultimate prophetic vision of the *Last Poems* is the subject of the
next essay.

III

LAPIS LAZULI AND THE MAN AND THE ECHO

•••

Lapis Lazuli

(FOR HARRY CLIFTON)

1. I have heard that hysterical women say
2. They are sick of the palette and fiddle-bow,
3. Of poets that are always gay,
4. For everyone knows or else should know
5. That if nothing drastic is done
6. Aeroplane and Zeppelin will come out,
7. Pitch like King Billy bomb-balls in
8. Until the town lie beaten flat.

9. All perform their tragic play,
10. There struts Hamlet, there is Lear,
11. That's Ophelia, that Cordelia;
12. Yet they, should the last scene be there,
13. The great stage curtain about to drop,
14. If worthy their prominent part in the play,
15. Do not break up their lines to weep.
16. They know that Hamlet and Lear are gay;
17. Gaiety transfiguring all that dread.
18. All men have aimed at, found and lost;
19. Black out; Heaven blazing into the head:
20. Tragedy wrought to its uttermost.
21. Though Hamlet rambles and Lear rages,
22. And all the drop-scenes drop at once
23. Upon a hundred thousand stages,
24. It cannot grow by an inch or an ounce.

25. On their own feet they came, or on shipboard,
26. Camel-back, horse-back, ass-back, mule-back,
27. Old civilizations put to the sword.
28. Then they and their wisdom went to rack:
29. No handiwork of Callimachus,
30. Who handled marble as if it were bronze,
31. Made draperies that seemed to rise
32. When sea-wind swept the corner, stands;
33. His long lamp-chimney shaped like the stem
34. Of a slender palm, stood but a day;
35. All things fall and are built again,
36. And those that build them again are gay.

37. Two Chinamen, behind them a third
38. Are carved in lapis lazuli,
39. Over them flies a long-legged bird,
40. A symbol of longevity;
41. The third, doubtless a serving man,
42. Carries a musical instrument.

43. Every discoloration of the stone,
44. Every accidental crack or dent,
45. Seems a water-course or an avalanche,
46. Or lofty slope where it still snows
47. Though doubtless plum or cherry-branch
48. Sweetens the little half-way house
49. Those Chinamen climb towards, and I
50. Delight to imagine them seated there;
51. There, on the mountain and the sky,
52. On all the.tragic scene they stare.
53. One asks for mournful melodies;
54. Accomplished fingers begin to play.
55. Their eyes mid many wrinkles, their eyes,
56. Their ancient, glittering eyes, are gay.

The Man and the Echo

MAN

1. In a cleft that's christened Alt
2. Under broken stone I halt
3. At the bottom of a pit
4. That broad noon has never lit,
5. And shout a secret to the stone.
6. All that I have said and done,
7. Now that I am old and ill,
8. Turns into a question till
9. I lie awake night after night
10. And never get the answers right.
11. Did that play of mine send out
12. Certain men the English shot?
13. Did words of mine put too great strain
14. On that woman's reeling brain?
15. Could my spoken words have checked
16. That whereby a house lay wrecked?
17. And all seems evil until I
18. Sleepless would lie down and die.

ECHO

19. Lie down and die.

MAN

That were to shirk
20. The spiritual intellect's great work,
21. And shirk it in vain. There is no release
22. In a bodkin or disease,
23. Nor can there be work so great

24. As that which cleans man's dirty slate.
25. While man can still his body keep
26. Wine or love drug him to sleep,
27. Waking he thanks the Lord that he
28. Has body and its stupidity,
29. But body gone he sleeps no more,
30. And till his intellect grows sure
31. That all's arranged in one clear view,
32. Pursues the thoughts that I pursue,
33. Then stands in judgment on his soul,
34. And, all work done, dismisses all
35. Out of intellect and sight
36. And sinks at last into the night.

ECHO

37. Into the night.

MAN

O Rocky Voice,
38. Shall we in that great night rejoice?
39. What do we know but that we face
40. One another in this place?
41. But hush, for I have lost the theme,
42. Its joy or night seem but a dream;
43. Up there some hawk or owl has struck,
44. Dropping out of sky or rock,
45. A stricken rabbit is crying out,
46. And its cry distracts my thought.

On 6 July 1935 Yeats wrote to Dorothy Wellesley:

People much occupied with morality always lose heroic ecstasy. Those who have it most often are those Dowson has described (I cannot find the poem but the lines run like this or something like this)

> Wine and women and song
> To us they belong
> To us the bitter and gay.

'Bitter and gay', that is the heroic mood.

Yeats would first have heard, or read, Dowson's 'Villanelle of the Poet's Road' in the days of the Rhymers' Club, and it is likely that it came to mind forty years later as a result of his reading for *The Oxford Book of Modern Verse*. In that anthology Dowson was to stand at its maker's right hand, his 'Villanelle' following Yeats's own 'From "Oedipus at Colonus" '. The fourth stanza of Dowson's poem provided, I think, the seed from which 'Lapis Lazuli' was to spring when in July 1936,[1] if we are to believe F. 1r of the manuscript, 'Some woman said to me yesterday, I am sick of . . . poets that seem always gay.' This idle remark must surely have reminded Yeats of Dowson's lines:

> Unto us they belong,
>   Us the bitter and gay,
> Wine and women and song.

The connection between 'Villanelle of the Poet's Road' and 'Lapis Lazuli' would seem to be clinched by a later paragraph of Yeats's letter of 6 July, in which Harry Clifton's gift is mentioned for the first time:

I notice that you have much lapis lazuli; someone has sent me a present of a great piece carved by some Chinese sculptor into the semblance of a mountain with temple, trees, paths and an ascetic and pupil about to

---

[1] On 26 July he wrote to Dorothy Wellesley: 'Yesterday I finished my longer poem "Lapis Lazuli".'

climb the mountain. Ascetic, pupil, hard stone, eternal theme of the sensual east. The heroic cry in the midst of despair. But no, I am wrong, the east has its solutions always and therefore knows nothing of tragedy. It is we, not the east, that must raise the heroic cry.

In Dowson's phrase 'bitter and gay' he finds 'the heroic mood' that is the antithesis of despair.

His meditative description of the lapis lazuli is much quoted but not always understood. Indeed, it is difficult to see what Yeats can have meant before he corrected himself; perhaps that the ascetic and pupil, representing the intellect, raise 'the heroic cry in the midst of despair' in their refusal to accept the apathy, indolence, and fatalism of 'the sensual east'. On second thoughts he rejects this interpretation, because the Oriental philosopher with his doctrines of predestination and reincarnation 'knows nothing of tragedy'. This Yeats might have defined as the death of a hero who, though physically overthrown, confronts the unknown with courage and a cheerful spirit, like Cuchulain or Major Robert Gregory. Having celebrated heroic man throughout his life, it is hardly surprising that in the poems of his later years he adopts this attitude towards his own death.[1]

Twelve months after he had first mentioned the carving to Dorothy Wellesley, it would seem that a woman's chance remark struck a spark of reaction in his mind by which he saw his way into the poem 'Lapis Lazuli'. Frank O'Connor gives a revealing account of other raw materials used in its composition:

> I went to see Yeats one night, very troubled by an unsatisfactory production of Lady Gregory's *Dervorgilla*, which had been spoiled for me because the heroine wept at the curtain. I put off speaking of it because I noticed on the mantel-piece a new acquisition; a beautiful piece of lapis carved with gay scenes of a Chinese pilgrimage. Yeats was very pleased with it and told me he was writing a poem to the man who had given it to him. Then he went on to tell me of a letter he had just received from Edmund Dulac, who was terrified of what was going to happen if London was bombed from the air. I told him of my own experience and asked, 'Is it ever permissible for an actor to sob at the curtain of a play?' and he replied, 'Never!'[2]

---

[1] For a perceptive discussion of Yeats's conception of heroic joy, with special reference to this poem, see Edward Engelberg, *The Vast Design | Patterns in W. B. Yeats's Aesthetic*, 1964, pp. 166–75.

[2] Frank O'Connor, *The Backward Look*, 1967, p. 174. Yeats returned to this subject in 'A General Introduction for my Work', written in 1937: 'no actress has ever sobbed when she

There are in the National Library of Ireland three lined, loose-leaf folios of manuscript and six quarto sheets of typescript; relatively small roots for so substantial a poem. Other drafts may have been lost or destroyed, though this is unlikely for the manuscript has the 'feel' of a poem that grew naturally and rapidly. Yeats wrote his first draft in ink, which he later corrected in pencil (represented in my transcription by bold italic). As often happened, he had difficulty in starting:

F. 1r: (.)
    I have heard that some queer women
    ~~*I know a dozen women that say*~~
  ~~*Some woman said to me yesterday,*~~
    They are
 ~~*I am*~~ *sick of the pallet & fiddle bow,*
   Or *and poets*
~~*I am sick of men*~~ *that seem always gay   should   now*
  ~~*For nothing else matters but know*~~ ~~*This can matter know that*~~ *we know*
~~*What matters now is a* (.   ) *& to show*~~

This line, that would seem to anticipate the insistent 'What matter' of 'The Gyres',[1] Yeats attempts again at the top of the page

           matters   **now that we**
   That nothing ~~*should matter now that*~~ *we know*
                     or should know

before moving on to the 'queer women's' vision of the outbreak of war.[2]

        someday soon
  That ~~*tomorrow or next day*~~ *war must begin*

  Aero planes (.   ) *over the* ~~*towns*~~ *town*

  Zeppalins throw their bomb balls in

  ~~*That nothing should be talked or done*~~
             (.)
  That nothing ~~*should*~~ *matter any more*

  But how to make an end of war

played Cleopatra, even the shallow brain of a producer has never thought of such a thing'. *Essays and Introductions*, 1961, p. 523.
  [1] Curtis Bradford dates the final draft of this poem 9 April 1937. See *Yeats at Work*, 1965, p. 142.
  [2] See pp. 153-4 for a similar vision in the cancelled drafts of 'Under Ben Bulben'.

Before populations are blotted out

Galleries ~~museum~~ *museum blown into the air*

Civilization beaten flat

As Jeffares points out, the Zeppelin, 'anachronistic for bombing purposes in 1936, is probably due to the poet's memories of air raids on London in the 1914–18 war',[1] revived by Dulac's letter. He traces the bomb-balls back to a stanza from 'The Battle of the Boyne', a ballad included in *Irish Minstrelsy*, an anthology edited by H. Halliday Sparling:

> King James has pitched his tent between
> The lines for to retire;
> But King William threw his bomb-balls in
> And set them all on fire.[2]

The echo is stronger than the original. As well as calling King William King Billy, a name more likely to stir up immediate historical and political memories and associations in an Irishman, Yeats took over the word 'pitch' and used it for the bomb-balls instead of the tent.[3]

Jeffares was more accurate than he knew, for F. 1r shows that Yeats originally wrote 'Zeppalins throw their bomb balls in'. His first draft continues with a metaphor that must surely derive from Shakespeare's 'All the world's a stage':

> *II*
>
> *Yet men   their*
> ~~*We all*~~ *perform our tragic plays*
> *This   this other*
> ~~*One*~~ *man* ~~*plays*~~ *Hamlet another Lear,*
> *Weep   weep*
> ~~*Wept*~~ *Opheleas, wept Cordeleas*

> *But we, should the last scene be there*

---

[1] The General and Particular Meanings of "Lapis Lazuli" ', Jon Stallworthy, ed., *Yeats: Last Poems*, 1968, p. 160.

[2] H. Halliday Sparling, ed., *Irish Minstrelsy*, 1888, p. 319. There is a copy of this anthology, inscribed by the editor, in Yeats's library. It contained a poem by Yeats, who probably first met Sparling at the house of William Morris. Cf. a passage from Elizabeth Yeats's diary for 1888–9, quoted by Joseph Hone, 'A Scattered Fair', *The Wind and the Rain* (Autumn 1946), p. 113.

[3] Jeffares, op. cit., p. 160.

The great stage curtain about to drop

If worthy our prominent part in the play

Do not break up our lines to weep
                                        are
Recall that Hamlet & Lear ~~were~~ gay
    That
Gaety transfiguring dread

Everything found, everything lost

Black out, heaven blazing into the head
   Tragedy wrought
~~Tragedy there~~ at its uttermost,
   (. .)*increase*
~~Not to be increased~~ by an inch or an ounce

      ~~Nor can it~~ increase ~~by~~ an inch or an ounce
      will   That cannot

I suspect that, having completed his rough draft of the poem
(F. 1r–F. 3r), Yeats went over it again making pencilled corrections
and cancelling lines 4–8 with diagonal strokes. Then it would seem
he took to his pen again, turned F. 1r on its side, and wrote along
the right-hand margin—over several faint lines of pencil that I cannot read—a revised version of lines 4–8:

   That everybody knows or else should know
     if nothing
   That ~~unless something~~ drastic is on

   The aero planes & Zeppelins will be out
    And   Like William
   ~~When they~~ have thrown their bomb balls in
   Until the town lie
   ~~Civilization~~ be beaten flat

The rapid movement of these lines and their colloquial diction—
'everybody', 'drastic', 'town' replacing 'Civilization'—give a more
convincing impression of cocktail-party prattle than before. Such
a context enables the poet to introduce his theme unobtrusively;
the poets' gaiety is condemned as frivolity, but the obvious irony of
this passage annuls the condemnation. At the same time, the
apparently casual insertion 'Like William' [of Orange at the Battle

of the Boyne] sounds the first note of his secondary theme, that of the cyclic recurrence of history. The break between the stanza paragraphs signals a change in tone, and the long, slow vowels with which the second opens indicate that now the poet is speaking *in propria persona*, answering the first speaker.

If I am right in thinking this the first draft, the poem unfolds with amazing authority. Its outline is firm from the start and, apart from the recasting of lines 1–8, there are no structural alterations. Certain of the minor changes, however, are interesting. The personal note in the original opening of the second paragraph is muted in successive revisions: 'We all perform' becoming 'We men perform' becoming 'Yet men perform'.[1] The tragic heroines are introduced, mis-spelt, and what Jeffares calls 'an implicit comparison' is made between them and the women, later described as hysterical, in line 1. Since Yeats goes on to say

> *But we, . . .*
>
> *If worthy our prominent part in the play*
>
> *Do not break up our lines to weep*

it is curious that the 'Opheleas' and 'Cordeleas' should at first be said to have wept, and more curious that they should then be instructed to weep.

Hamlet and Lear at this point make their first appearance in Yeats's poetry, though both are to be found in his prose. At school, he tells us, Shakespeare was 'read . . . for his grammar exclusively', but J. B. Yeats clearly corrected this imbalance in his son's education at home.[2]

When I was ten or twelve my father took me to see Irving play Hamlet, and did not understand why I preferred Irving to Ellen Terry, who was, I can now see, the idol of himself and his friends. I could not think of her, as I could of Irving's Hamlet, as but myself, and I was not old enough to care for feminine charm and beauty. For many years Hamlet was an image of heroic self-possession for the poses of youth and childhood to copy, a combatant of the battle within myself.[3]

---

[1] For a similar movement from the subjective to the objective, see Jon Stallworthy, *Between the Lines*, pp. 246–8.

[2] *Autobiographies*, 1955, pp. 57–8.

[3] Ibid., p. 47.

Hamlet figures prominently in Yeats's essay on Shakespeare, 'At Stratford-on-Avon', written in 1901, and the portraits of him in his twenties and thirties leave one in little doubt as to the Prince of Denmark's influence on his dress and manner. Not surprisingly, Lear would seem to have interested him less as a young man; reading that play in later life, the image of his grandfather was always before him;[1] and 'at life's end' he was to write:

> Grant me an old man's frenzy,
> Myself must I remake
> Till I am Timon and Lear
> Or that William Blake
> Who beat upon the wall
> Till truth obeyed his call;

In the shadow of death 'Hamlet and Lear are gay', as Yeats himself sought to be, though at a time of ill health he wrote to Dorothy Wellesley: 'I thought my problem was to face death with gaiety, now I have learnt that it is to face life.'[2] The powerful paradoxical image of 'heaven blazing into the head' as all earthly concerns black out, operates both on theatrical and philosophical levels. It suggests at once the sudden blaze of house-lights as the foot-lights 'black out' and the Neoplatonic concept referred to on page 38.

The first draft continues on F. 2r:

> *If*
> ~~*Though*~~ *Hamlet rambles, and Lear rages*
> *the*
> *And all ~~those~~ drop scenes drop at once*
>
> *Upon a hundred thousand stages*

Dr. Oliver Edwards has pointed out to me that the prophetic element in this apocalyptic image was fulfilled at Hiroshima and Nagasaki when 'the fringed curtains of [the] eye' dropped at once upon one hundred and twenty thousand stages.

From his expanding metaphor of the 'tragic play', Yeats moves

[1] Ibid., p. 9.
[2] Dorothy Wellesley, ed., *Letters on Poetry from W. B. Yeats to Dorothy Wellesley*, 1964, p. 149. All subsequent quotations from this book are taken from the 1964 paperback reissue, introduced by Kathleen Raine.

in the third stanza-paragraph to the raw material of tragedy, history, and significantly his starting-point is Troy:

III

In wooden horses, in chariots ~~on~~ ship board

Camel back, horse back, ass back, mule back

They came & multitudes put to the sword

Old civilizations brought to wrack .
* The*
The handy work of Kallimicos
* handled*
Who ~~handled~~ marble as if it were bronze
* when the wind*
His draperies, that ~~seemed~~ to rise

When wind rose at the corner stands
The long *   his long   chimney*   *the stem*
~~Not that~~ lamp ~~chimney sta~~ shaped like ~~a pa~~
Yet he *   (. . . .)   ~~that has had its day~~*
Of a slender palm, ~~that was praised for a day~~ lived but a day

All things fall flat & are built ~~up~~ up again

And those that build them again are gay

Dissatisfied with lines 31 and 32 he drafted them again on F. 1*v*:

*   when the wind rose*
Those draperies that seemed ~~to rise~~

And (.)
*   seemed when the wind rose*
Made draperies that ~~seemed to rise~~

(. .) there when

To billow or (.) stand

Below this he wrote, presumably to clarify his rhyme-scheme:

bronze

stands

bronze

marble

'Lapis Lazuli' began with 'some woman's' criticism of artists fiddling as the world is about to burn; a criticism that the poet-playwright rejected in his image of life as tragic theatre. His subsequent reverie on the tragic past, 'multitudes put to the sword', counterpoints the woman's earlier vision of the tragic future; just as his introduction of 'Kallimicos' counterpoints the earlier mention of artists 'that are always gay'. Yeats almost certainly read of Callimachus' 'draperies' and 'long lamp chimney' in *Pausanias's Description of Greece*, translated with a commentary by J. G. Frazer. Pausanias is mentioned in *A Vision*:

With Callimachus pure Ionic revives again, as Furtwängler has proved, and upon the only example of his work known to us, a marble chair, a Persian is represented, and may one not discover a Persian symbol in that bronze lamp, shaped like a palm, known to us by a description in Pausanias? But he was an archaistic workman, and those who set him to work brought back public life to an older form. One may see in masters and man a momentary dip into ebbing Asia.[1]

Writing in what Frazer calls the 'mellow autumn . . . of the ancient world, when the last gleanings of the Greek genius were being gathered in,' Pausanias speaks of

an image of Athena in what is now called the Acropolis, but what was then called the city. The legend is that the image fell from heaven, but whether this was so or not I will not inquire. Callimachus made a golden lamp for the goddess. They fill the lamp with oil, and wait till the same day next year, and the oil suffices for the lamp during all the intervening time, though it is burning day and night. The wick is made of Carpasian flax, which is the only kind of flax that does not take fire. A bronze palm-tree placed over the lamp and reaching to the roof draws off the smoke. Callimachus, who made the lamp, though inferior to the best artists in the actual practice of his art, so far surpassed them all in ingenuity, that he was the first to bore holes in stones, and assumed, or accepted at the hands of others, the title of the Refiner away of Art.[2]

In a note on this passage Frazer writes that

The date of this artist is not positively known; but as it seems probable that he made the golden lamp for the new Erechtheum at the time of its

---

[1] *A Vision*, 1937, p. 270. See also 'The Cutting of an Agate', *Essays and Introductions*, p. 225.

[2] J. G. Frazer, trans., *Pausanias's Description of Greece*, 1898, vol. i, p. 39. I am indebted to Mr. William St. Clair for guiding me to this work.

completion about 408 B.C., he may have flourished at the end of the fifth century B.C. . . . . Perhaps Callimachus may have used the borer in a way unknown to his predecessors as for the making of fine grooves and deep under-cuttings in imitating the folds and creases of drapery and the wavy ripples of hair, where the chisel could not have answered his purpose. We learn from Pliny (*N.H.* xxxiv. 92) that the epithet 'Refiner away of Art' was applied to Callimachus on account of his excessive fastidiousness which impelled him to touch and retouch his work without end. Pliny mentions as an instance a group of dancing Laconian girls by Callimachus; the work was free from any technical faults, but so over elaborated that all ease and grace were lost. Vitruvius says (iv. 1. 9) that the title in question was bestowed on Callimachus by the Athenians on account of 'the elegance and subtlety' of his work in marble.[1]

Yeats's statement that the 'long lamp-chimney . . . stood but a day' is almost certainly his own addition, since when Pausanias saw it it had already been standing for over 550 years and probably survived until the Goths sacked Athens in A.D. 267. *Sub specie aeternitatis*, however, this is 'but a day'.

Callimachus, Yeats implies, was gay; and even in their rough form, with the word 'flat' in line 35 echoing temporarily its first use in line 8, the lines that end stanza-paragraph III have a confident gaiety that embodies Yeats's statement of his theme:

> *All things fall flat & are built ~~up~~ up again*

> *And those that build them again are gay* [.]

He builds his poem gaily, untroubled by the thought that it, too, may 'stand but a day'. The transition from the handiwork of the Greek sculptor to that of the Chinese is made without a word of explanation; simply with the space between paragraphs. A jump so daring could only be brought off by a master poet at the height of his confident powers. He outstrides his readers, but knows he has them on a leash.

IV

> *Two ~~Chin~~ Chinamen behind them a third*

> *Are carved in ~~lapis lazuli~~ lapis lazuli*

[1] Ibid., vol. ii, p. 342.

> *legged*
> *Over them flies a long ~~lived~~ bird*
>
> *A symbol of longevity,*
>
> *The third doubtless a serving man*
>
> *Carries a musical instrument.*
>
> *Every discolourization of the stone*
>
> *Every accidental crack or dent*
>
> *Seems ~~a~~ water course or avalanche*
>   *a*
>
> *Or lofty slope where it still snows*
>
> *Though doubtless plum or cherry branch*
>
> *Sweetens the little half way house*

F. 3r:

> *The old men climb towards & I*
>
> *Delight to imagine them seated there,*
>
> *Where the mountain & sky*
>   *There on the*
> *~~Upon~~ the tragic scene they stare;*
>
> *One asks for mournful melodies*
>
>   *s*
> *~~An old voice sings, and old hand plays play~~*
>   *Their eyes mid   wrinkles*
> *Their eyes amid many wrinkles, their eyes*
>
> *Their ancient glittering eyes are gay*
>
> *Accomplished fingers begin to play*
>
> *~~A skilled voice sings, and skilled hands play~~*

Two of the Chinamen, we know from Yeats's letter to Dorothy Wellesley, he identified as ascetic and pupil. His ascetic, like himself and indeed like all his sages, hermits, and wise men, is old. In both Chinese and Japanese art the long-legged crane appears as 'a symbol of longevity' from early medieval times onward. Yeats

E

identifies the third Chinaman, with more than a hint of patrician
hauteur, as 'doubtless a serving man' from his inferior position.
However, before attempting to draw any deductions about Yeats's
social attitudes from this passage, one should remember that he
probably identified himself equally with ascetic, disciple, and
musician. As Keats momentarily enters the scene depicted on the
Grecian urn, so Yeats climbs with his Chinamen their snow-
bright, blossom-bright mountain. He 'delights' to imagine them
staring 'On all the tragic scene'; that the scene *is* tragic does
not annul his delight. Their reaction is to ask for the 'mournful
melodies' heard in the closing scene of so many stage tragedies.[1]
As Keats's imagination conjures music from the marble
'pipes and timbrels', Yeats's accomplished fingers bring the lapis
lazuli to life, and his melody is far from mournful. The effect
of that adjective is cancelled by the excited triple repetition of
the last two lines and the triumphant conviction of the final
word:

> *Their eyes mid   wrinkles*
> *Their eyes amid many wrinkles, their eyes*
>
> ***Their ancient glittering eyes are gay***

The cyclic pattern celebrated in 'Lapis Lazuli' is cunningly
reinforced by the ancient Chinaman's musical instrument which,
by association, confers a new dignity on the modern fiddle-bow so
contemptuously dismissed in the opening lines.

F. 3r is completed by two stanzas presumably translated from the
Gaelic ballad that provided Yeats with a refrain for 'The Three
Bushes'.[2]

> *'I know a girl' said I*
>
> *(O the brown & the yellow beer)*
>
> *Who can shorten the time of the sun & the clock*
>
> *(O my dear, O my dear)*

---

[1] See the final stage-directions of *The King's Threshold*—'*Some play a mournful music*';
and *The Death of Cuchulain*—'*Music from pipe and drum*'.

[2] See p. 81.

'So you may like the lower'

(O the brown & the yellow beer)

And I shall like the upper road

(O my dear O my dear)

The complete typescript of 'Lapis Lazuli'—so titled for the first time—begins with F. 4r. The corrections are in ink.

Lapis Lazuli

hysterical
I have heard that ~~some queer~~ women say

They are sick of the palette and fiddle-bow,
  O
~~And~~ of poets that are always gay,

That everybody knows or else should know
    is can be
That if nothing drastic ~~is~~ done,
       come   *come*
Areoplane and Zeppelin will ~~be~~ out
Pitch ~~Throw like~~ King Billy ~~drop~~
 ~~Like William throw their~~ bomb-balls in
Pitch
Until the town lie beaten flat.

All the inked corrections but one are improvements. The introduction of 'hysterical' tells the reader at once what he needs to know of the women; 'will come out' is both more accurate and more menacing than 'will be out'; 'Pitch' is more graphic than 'Throw' and has inflammatory associations; but, on the other hand, the colloquial rhythm of

   That if nothing drastic is done

is wholly lost once the line is changed to

   That if nothing drastic can be done

All the corrections to the second stanza-paragraph are improvements; the most important being the alteration of 'we' to 'they'

in line 12, and the two changes of 'our' to 'their' in lines 14
and 15.

> *All men*
> ~~Yet all~~ perform their tragic plays,
>
> This man Hamlet that other Lear,
>
> Weep, Ophelias, weep Cordelias
> *Yet they,* ~~if~~ *should*
> ~~But we should~~ the last scene be there
>
> The great stage curtain about to drop,
> *a their*
> If worthy ~~our~~ prominent part in the play,
> *their*
> Do do break up ~~our~~ lines to weep.
> *They know   are*
> ~~Recall~~ that Hamlet and Lear ~~were~~ gay,
>
> A gaiety transfiguring dread,
> *All men aimed at* ⟨ . ⟩ *found &*
> ~~Everything found, everything~~ lost
>
> Black out, Heaven blazing into the head;
> *wraught to*
> Tragedy ~~there at~~ its uttermost,
> *Though*
> Nor ~~can it increase an inch or an ounce~~
> *Though*
> *Though* ~~If~~ Hamlet rambles or Lear rages   *stet*
>
> And all the drop scenes drop at once
>
> F. 5*r*:   Upon the hundred thousand stages
>
> *It cannot grow by an inch or an ounce.*
>
>
> *on*
> In wooden horses, chariots, on shipboard,
>
> Camel-back, horse-back, ass-back, mule-back
>
> They came, and multitudes put to the sword
>
> Old civilizations brought to rack.

No handiwork of Calimachus

Who handled marble as if it were bronze—
    ~~Those~~ *Made*
The draperies that seemed to rise,
        sea wind swept
When ~~wind rose at~~ the corner, —~~stands~~ stands. ,

His long lamp chimney shaped like the stem
            stood but a
Of a slender palm ~~has had its~~ day.

All things fall ~~flat~~ and are built up again

And those that build them again are gay

Two Chinamen, behind them a third

Are carved in lapis lazuli,

Over them flies a long-legged bird

A symbol of longevity;

The third, doubtless a serving man

Carries a musical instrument

Every discolourisation of the stone

Every accidental crack or dent

Seems a water-course or an avalanche

Or lofty slope where it still snows

Though doubtless plum or cherry branch

Sweeten the little half way house
        Those Chinamen
F. 6r: ~~The old men~~ climb towards, and I
            to
Delight ~~to~~ imagine them seated there.

There, on the mountain and the sky,

On all the tragic scene they stare;

One asks for mournful melodies,

Accomplished fingers begin to play

Their eyes mid many wrinkles, their eyes,
T
their ancient, glittering eyes, are gay.

W. B. Yeats

Two small but significant changes are introduced between manuscript and typescript to give lines 29 and 51 their final form, but
'Sweetens' in line 48 is altered, perhaps accidentally, to 'Sweeten'.
Only when he comes to revise his typescript does Yeats give the
poem any punctuation to speak of. At this stage his pen makes a
number of other corrections, in addition to those already mentioned,
to finalize the wording of lines 16, 20, 24, 31, 32, 34, 35, 45, and 49.
In the last of these, by altering 'The old men' to 'Those Chinamen',
he jettisons an adjective that had appeared three times in the manuscript draft of this stanza-paragraph: 'old men', 'old voice', 'old
hands'. Perhaps he wished to avoid any suggestion of infirmity.
That their eyes are ancient is offset by their glitter.

F. 7r is a carbon copy of F. 4r on which line 18, having advanced
from
> Everything found, everything lost

to
> All men aimed at, found and lost

reaches its final form,
> All men have aimed at, found and lost

except for punctuation. F. 8r is a carbon copy of F. 6r that adds
nothing to the development of the poem. F. 9r is a later typescript
of lines 1–36 on which the dedication '(*For Harry Clifton*)' appears
for the first time and seven more lines are in tune. The opening of
the second stanza-paragraph is now dramatic, the poet pointing out
his dramatis personae:

> All perform their tragic play,

> There struts Hamlet, there is Lear,

> That's Ophelia, that Cordelia;

Line 15 has its 'not'; the buoyant movement of 'Gaiety trans-figuring' in line 17 is now balanced by the sombre stresses of 'all that dread'; wooden horse and chariot have been dropped from line 25 in favour of 'On their own feet they came'; 'Old civilizations' are moved back from line 28 to 27, and line 28 is recast as

> Then they or their wisdom went to rack:

Apart from changes in punctuation, four more alterations were made to the poem before its first printing, in *The London Mercury* (March 1938):

Line 21. . . . or Lear rages *becomes* . . . and Lear rages,

28. . . . or their wisdom . . . *becomes* . . . and their wisdom . . .

35. . . . built up again *becomes* . . . built again

43. . . . discolourisation . . . *becomes* . . . discoloration . . .

At a later printing, 'can be done' in line 5 became 'is done'; and 'Sweeten' in line 48 became 'Sweetens'. The few additional changes of spelling and punctuation are set out in the *Variorum* and need not be listed here.

Recreating in words the carving of lapis lazuli, Yeats communicates the delight that, he implies, the sculptor knew as he gave the Chinamen their 'ancient, glittering eyes'; and the revisions of this poem show him consistently pointing up the muscular gaiety of the rhythms that proclaim his theme.

2

The confident prophetic voice of 'Lapis Lazuli' is not, however, the only voice of Yeats's *Last Poems*. A striking contrast to the message proclaimed by Old Rocky Face and the Chinamen on their bright mountain top is the more private voice heard in 'The Man and the Echo', a poem probably started in July 1938.[1] Among the Yeats manuscripts in the National Library of Ireland are four large loose-leaf sheets, and two smaller ones, containing hand-written

---

[1] A version, 'Copied at Penns' and dated July 1938, appears in *Letters on Poetry*, pp. 179–81.

drafts of this poem; together with four complete typescripts, each
on two quarto sheets of typing paper.

'The Man and the Echo', like so many of Yeats's poems, began
with a prose draft—in places tantalizingly illegible—that shows
him making a first, tentative exploration of his theme:

Poet

F. 1v:[1]   *I stand in this dark alt, this mountain gash*

Cliff upon cliff, standing among the rocks,

My (.   .   .   ) words my books & words

All that I have done seems evil, seems

Like (.   .   ) that the ~~(.   .   )~~

by
Some where among this cliff ~~& think~~ *in vain*
~~*Worn down*~~
~~*Worn down by my self torturing search*~~

~~*Seek escape*~~

escape
Among this solitude I seek ~~*remorse*~~

From this self torture am I sick in mind

The alt, an Irish word for cliff, is identified by Jeffares as 'a rocky
fissure on Ben Bulben';[2] and by Sheelah Kirby as 'a deep chasm
one mile long and only thirty feet broad, bounded on each side by
steep cliffs and overgrown with trees and shrubs', on the south-west
of Knocknarea.[3] Yeats's reference to 'cliff upon cliff' in his prose
draft suggests that Mrs. Kirby is right. Old Rocky Face and the
Chinamen may stare on a tragic scene, but they have a field of vision
so wide that they can see beyond tragedy; whereas the Poet who
comes to the dark alt, as a questioner to the chasm at Delphi, comes
in search of illumination. For the moment he can see neither forward nor back.

F. 2r contains a draft of the last four lines of 'Crazy Jane on the

---

[1] F. 1r contains a draft of stanza III of 'The Statues': see p. 134.
[2] *Poems of W. B. Yeats*, 1962, p. 258.
[3] *The Yeats Country*, 1962, p. 27.

Mountain', though I think it not beyond the bounds of possibility that these began as part of the poet's meditation in the alt:

> ~~Thereon I fell on my knees~~
>
> ~~And~~ *I kissed a stone*
>
> *I lay stretched out in the dirt*
>
> *And I cried tears down*

Though the alt is a great distance from Blarney Castle, it is hard to see what, other than the Blarney Stone, Yeats can have had in mind when he wrote this quatrain.

On F. 2*v* he translates his prose draft into doggerel rhyme:

> *Here among tumbled of a Alt*
>
> *That narrowed the sky in a slit I halt*
>
> *That I may talk to the echo but first*
>
> *Because in grave dead look their worst*
>
> ~~For I am out of sorts I stand~~
>
> *For I am out of health stand dumb*
>   *has*
> *If any good thing, ever ~~came~~ come*
>   *work*
> *From ~~day~~ of mine I have ~~for~~ forgot*
>
> *I ask if such a man that soldier shot*
>
> *Went out because of ~~anything word of mine~~ such a word*
>
> *Then other dead come up*

The reference to the dead in the grave adds a new dimension to the poem. Though it would seem to be these that he is about to question,[1] he is himself old and 'out of health' and clearly the alt has put him in mind of his own grave. To this extent 'The Man and the Echo' may be regarded as a forerunner of 'Under Ben Bulben' (written one month later) in which Yeats speaks explicitly from his grave at the foot of the mountain.

---

[1] The supposed burial place of Queen Maeve is only a bowshot from the alt on Knocknarea.

The title of the poem appears for the first time on F. 3*r*, 'Poet' having been changed to 'Man'. Though it is the possible effects of his play *Cathleen Ni Houlihan*, first performed in April 1902 with Maud Gonne in the title-role, that most trouble his conscience and bring him to the alt, the metaphysical questions that his poem ultimately asks are relevant to all men, not only poets.

Man and Echo

The Man

In the broken stone of an Alt

Where skies a narrow slit I walk

And shout a secret to the stone

~~Now that I am old & ill~~

All that I have said & done

Dissatisfied with these lines, he recasts them on the right-hand side of the page:

The Alt

Whose names this singular spot

Now on broken stone I halt

At the bottom of a pit

That broad noon had lit

And shout my secret to the stone

The 'broken stone' transferred from line 1 to its final position in line 2 echoes line 1 of section VII of 'Meditations in Time of Civil War':

> I climb to the tower-top and lean upon broken stone,

The secret that he shouts must, I think, be the suspicion that he and his work 'have done but harm'; a private fear far removed from his more public celebrations of the artist's role as architect of civilization. F. 3*r* continues:

I seem Now that I am old & ill

Seems to have done but harm until

I lie awake night after night

And never get the answer right

Did that play of mine send out

Certain men the English shot

Or did my spoken words perplex

That man that woman now a wreck

I say that I have done some good

As well as evil but in this mood

I see but evil until I

Sleepless would lie down & die

Echo

Lie down & die

The Man

That were to shirk

The spiritual intellect's great work

And shirk it in vain. There's no release

In a bodkin or disease

Nor can there be a work so great

As that which cleans man's dirty slate

F. 4r: *While man can still his body keep*

~~*So long as man to body keeps*~~ *Wine or love drug him to sleep*
                         ~~*to body*~~
~~*While a man his body keeps keeps*~~

~~*By wine or women drugged he sleeps*~~
         Waking he
~~*And wakening*~~ *thanks the lord that he*

Has body & its stupidity

But body gone he sleeps no more
                  thing's
~~*Till every thing's convinced & sure*~~

~~*Till his mind is*~~ *convinced & sure*

~~*That what it thinks of life is true*~~

Pursues the thoughts that I pursue
          he being satisfied blots
Then ~~*satisfied at last*~~ *drives all*
                        ~~*its*~~
Human existence from ~~*his*~~/*sight   his*

And sinks at last into the night

                Echo

Into the night

            The Man

                O rocky void

Shall we in that great night rejoice

What do we know but that we face

One another in this place.

~~*Up there Hawk hawk*~~
                    Up there
~~*Up there*~~ *some hawk or owl has struck*

Dropping out of sky or rock

A stricken rabbit is crying out

And its cry distracts my thought

To the right of this draft Yeats re-works lines 30–5:

~~*And until his mind is sure*~~

~~*And he until his mind is sure*~~

~~*And until mind's*~~

That its vision of life is true
Thinks   And   stand stand out
And all things stand until

Pursue the thing that I pursue:

Pronounces judgement on the soul

(.   .   .   ) blots it all

Out of mind & out of sight

Then stands in judgement on his soul

And all work done dismisses all

Out of mind & out of sight

The poem's outline is now complete. The Man, struggling with his troubled recollections of *Cathleen Ni Houlihan* and Margot Ruddock,[1] is answered by the Echo that voices his own despair: 'Lie down & die'. This dialogue between the forces of Life and Death, 'To be or not to be', reminds him of Hamlet and the 'bare bodkin'. There would seem to be another Shakespearian association, this time from Macbeth,[2] in the line: 'But body gone he sleeps no more'. The meaning of this difficult sentence is to some extent clarified by Book III of *A Vision* (1937 edition), which is entitled significantly 'The Soul in Judgement' and describes the six states between death and re-birth. In the second of these states,

the *Return*, . . . the *Spirit* must live through past events in the order of their occurrence, because it is compelled by the *Celestial Body* to trace every passionate event to its cause until all are related and understood, turned into knowledge, made a part of itself.[3]

The *Spirit* is still unsatisfied, until after the third state, which corresponds to Gemini, called the Shiftings, where the Spirit is purified of good and evil.[4]

The verbal echoes of *A Vision* in 'The Man and the Echo' remind us that the poem was written less than a year after the second edition of the book was published.

---

[1] See 'A Crazed Girl' and Yeats's Introduction to her book of poems, *The Lemon Tree*, 1937.   [2] Act II, scene 2, line 44: 'Macbeth shall sleep no more!'
[3] p. 226.   [4] p. 231.

Yeats, in the tomb-like alt tracing 'every passionate event to its cause', thus anticipates his death, but even the consolation of this afterlife is denied him by the despairing Echo: 'Into the night'. Refusing to accept its grim conclusion he throws back, in a beseeching question, the word 'night' that the Echo had thrown at him:

> *O rocky void*
>
> *Shall we in that great night rejoice [?]*
>
> *What do we know but that we face*
>
> *One another in this place.*

Is the hereafter, he asks, not as he had depicted it in 'Mohini Chatterjee', for example:

> Old lovers yet may have
> All that time denied—
> Grave is heaped on grave
> That they be satisfied—

May not the loved and familiar dead only be waiting for his death to reveal themselves? Before the Echo can reply, a stricken animal cries out, and one wonders whether Yeats may not have had at the back of his mind an incident described in *Autobiographies*:

I fished for pike at Castle Dargan and shot at birds with a muzzle-loading pistol until somebody shot a rabbit and I heard it squeal. From that on I would kill nothing but the dumb fish.[1]

There is also a resemblance, probably no more than coincidental, to James Stephens's best-known poem, 'The Snare':

> I hear a sudden cry of pain!
>   There is a rabbit in a snare:
> Now I hear the cry again,
>   But I cannot tell from where.

Vivienne Koch sees the cry of the stricken rabbit as 'the answer to the pit, to negation, and to the rocky voice of Echo';[2] but this is to rob the poem of an ambiguity that must, surely, be deliberate. That Yeats receives no answer to his question does not mean, I think, that Echo is silenced. Their dialogue is simply interrupted by the cry

---

[1] p. 55.   [2] *W. B. Yeats / The Tragic Phase*, 1951, p. 120.

of the dying rabbit that inevitably puts the poet in mind of his own death. In other words, a natural horror at the thought of dying distracts him from speculation on what follows the moment of death. Though I believe Yeats's question is unanswered, the rabbit's cry does more to confirm than to deny the Echo's grim conclusion.

Having finished his rough draft (or perhaps in the middle of it), he made two further corrections, the first on F. 5*v* to lines 15–17:

> Could my spoken words have checked
> wrecked
> ~~That whereby a house was w~~

> Those events that a house wreck

> It seems that all etc

On F. 6*r* he experimented with lines 17 and 18:[1]

> It seems that all was well could I

> A withered man lie down & die

At this point the poem advanced into typescript. F. 7*r* and F. 8*r* have both ink and pencil corrections:

Man and Echo

The Man

In the broken stone of the Alt

Where sky's a narrow slit I ~~walk~~ *halt*

And shout a secret to~~t~~ the stone:

'All that I have said and done

Now that I am old and ill
                    Start questions in the night
~~Seems to have done but harm~~ until
                         ~~(.) *me with remorse*~~
I lie awake night after night.   ~~start questions in my soul~~

I| ~~And~~ never get the answer/right. |*s   on the night*

---

[1] F. 6*v* contains a draft of one of the 'Three Songs to One Burden'.

Did that play of mine send out

Certain men the English shot?

did ~~Or do my spoken words perplex~~ *Could my spoken words have*
checked

That man, that woman ~~now a wreck~~?   *that was wrecked*

I say that I have done some good

As well as evil, but in this mood

I see but evil until I

Sleepless would lie down and die.

Echo

Lie down and die.

The Man

That were to shirk

The spiritual intellect's great work

And shirk it in vain. There's no release

In a bodkin or disease,

Nor can there be work so great

As that which cleans man's dirty slate₍,₎:

While man can still his body keep

Wine or love drug/   him to sleep;   /s

Waking he thanks the Lord that he

Has body and its stupidity,

But body gone he sleeps no more,

Until/

~~And so unless his mind is sure~~

~~That its vision of life is true~~   ~~That all stands out in one~~
~~clear view~~

~~Pursues the thoughts that I pursue;~~   ~~Then stands in judge-~~
~~ment on his soul~~

~~Then he being satisfied blots out~~   *~~And all work done dis-~~*
                                                  ~~misses all~~

~~Human existence from his sight~~   *~~Out of sight mind & out~~*
                                                  ~~of sight~~

And sinks at last into the night.

Echo   *And till intellect grow*
                                          sure

Into the night.   *That all's arranged in*
                                     one clear view

~~The Man~~   *Pursues the ~~th~~ thing that*
                                     I pursue
                      Then stands in judge-
                                 ment on the soul
                      And all work done dis-
                                    misses all
                      Out of mind & out of
                                          sight

F. 8*r*:   The Man

                O rocky ~~void~~   *ce|*

Shall we in this great night rejoice?

What do we know but that we face

One another in this place?

Up there some hawk or owl has struck

Dropping out of sky or rock.

A stricken rabbit/crying out   *is|*

And its cry distracts my thought.

Below this Yeats strikes out a new couplet to be inserted, as is indicated by a swirling arrow, after line 40:

    But hush for I have lost the theme

    Its joy or night seem but a dream [.]

There are some interesting advances here:

   Line 5. . . . my secret . . . *has become* . . . a secret . . .

      8. Seems to have done but harm until
         becomes
         Start questions in the night until

F

Line 10. . . . answer . . . *becomes* . . . answers . . .

15. Or did my spoken words perplex
becomes
Could my spoken word have checked

16. . . . now a wreck? *becomes* . . . that was wrecked?

23. . . . a work . . . *has become* . . . work . . .

30–6. And so unless his mind is sure
That its vision of life is true
Pursues the thoughts that I pursue;
Then he being satisfied blots out
Human existence from his sight
And sinks at last into the night.

These lines, after some jottings that largely repeat F. 4r, *leap to almost their final form:*

And till intellect grow sure
That all's arranged in one clear view
Pursues the thing that I pursue
Then stands in judgement on the soul
And all work done dismisses all
Out of mind *&* out of sight
[And sinks at last into the night.]

37. . . . void *becomes* . . . voice

38. . . . that great night . . . *reverts to* . . . this great night . . .

41–2. But hush for I have lost the theme
Its joy or night seem but a dream

spring, fully-formed, into the poem.

This last addition—with its balancing of 'joy or night' against the 'night' and 'rejoice' of line 38, and its slightly hypnotic internal rhyme 'seem but a dream'—points up the transition from the dream of death to the reality.

The version of 'The Man and the Echo' that Yeats copied out for Dorothy Wellesley at Penns in the Rocks in July 1938 is basically that of this first typescript. It incorporates his manuscript corrections to lines 2, 10, and 45 (an obvious mis-typing), but not those to lines 8, 15, 30–5, 37, 41, and 42. The second typescript (F. 9r and F. 10r), which is dated 12 August, marks an intermediate stage.

'The Man' is corrected to 'Man' and certain lines are altered but do not reach their final form:

Line 1. . . . the Alt *has become* . . . an alt

Lines 16*a* and *b*. I say that I have done some good
As well as evil, but in this mood
are cancelled.

Lines 17 and 18. I see but evil until I
Sleepless would lie down and die.
are cancelled and recast as:

~~*And it seems that all were well if I*~~

~~*So withered could lie down and die*~~
could
And it seems that all was well ~~if~~ I
A withered man,
~~*Could there upon*~~ *lie down & die*

The adjective 'withered' recalls 'old wrinkled Rocky Face' of 'The Gyres' and the Chinamen's 'eyes mid many wrinkles'.

This typescript has one notable manuscript addition:

Lines 13 and 14. *Did words of mine lay too great strain*

On that woman's reeling brain [?]

The rhetorical repetition of 'Did' suggests the relentless questioning of his conscience. While 'that great night' is restored in line 38, 'answers' reverts to 'answer' in line 10, and the redundant indefinite article is reintroduced between 'be' and 'work' in line 23. Lines 30–6 barely consolidate the advance made on F. 7*r*, appearing on F. 9*r* as:

Till spiritual intellect is|	*intellect grow*|
~~And until his mind~~ is sure	
That all ~~starts out~~ in one clear view,	*s'arranged*|
Pursues the thoughts that I pursue,	
Then stands in judgment on his soul	
work| And all ~~work~~ done, dismisses all	
Out of mind and out of sight	
And sinks at last into the night.	

The third typescript (F. 11*r* and F. 12*r*) is a carbon copy of the second and is dated 30 August. Nine lines here attain their final shape in manuscript corrections:

Lines 1–4. In a cleft that's christened Alt

Under broken stone I halt

At the bottom of a pit

~~Broad~~ That broad noon has never lit,

Line 8.   Turns into a question till

13.   Did words of mine put too great strain

16.   That whereby a house was wrecked[1]

17.   And all seems evil until I

35.   Out of intellect and sight

No advances are made on the fourth typescript (F. 13*r* and F. 14*r*), but Yeats altered one word and added another for the poem's first printing in *The Atlantic Monthly* (January 1939):

Line 10. . . . answer . . . *became* . . . answers . . .

30. And till intellect . . . *became* And till his intellect . . .

Having seen it in print he made two further alterations, apart from changes of punctuation, for its second printing in *The London Mercury* (also January 1939):

Line 16. . . . was wrecked? *became* . . . lay wrecked?

26. . . . drugs him . . . *became* . . . drug him . . .

The indefinite article in line 23 appeared in *Last Poems and Two Plays* (1939), but not in *Last Poems and Plays* (1940).

In the earlier book, where the sequence of poems followed a list of contents found among Yeats's papers at his death,[2] 'The Man and the Echo' preceded 'The Circus Animals' Desertion' to which

---

[1] A reference to Coole.

[2] See Curtis Bradford, 'Yeats's "Last Poems" Again', No. viii of the *Dolmen Press Yeats Centenary Papers*, 1965.

it is thematically related. The Echo's 'Lie down and die' is linked
to the poet's

> I must lie down where all the ladders start,
> In the foul rag and bone shop of the heart.

He intended 'The Circus Animals' Desertion' to be followed (and,
presumably, his *Collected Poems* ended) by 'Politics'; the reference
to himself when young, 'starved for the bosom of [Oisin's] faery
bride' linking with his last, passionate exclamation:

> But O that I were young again
> And held her in my arms!

The delicate balance of the *Last Poems* was lost when the poems that
made up this poignant finale were reshuffled by Yeats's publishers
after his death and replaced by the confident rhetoric of 'Under
Ben Bulben'.

The pattern of disappointment and disapproval that greeted the
altered style of *The Green Helmet and Other Poems* (1910) and
Responsibilities (1914) was to some extent repeated in the critical
reception of *Last Poems and Two Plays* (1939) and *Last Poems and
Plays* (1940). Most reviewers found these lacking 'the brilliance
and profusion of *The Tower* and *The Winding Stair* (presumably
his best books, certainly the ones which crystallized the superiority
of his late work over his earlier)',[1] and F. R. Leavis considered the
1940 volume 'saddening', on account of its 'slackening . . . tension',
'bitterness and an agonized sense of frustrate impotence'.[2] Though
few would now deny that Yeats's critics were nearer the mark in
1939–40 than they were in 1910–14, in both periods they condemned him for not doing what he had done before (assuming he
could no longer do it) and overlooked the possibility that he might
be trying to do something else.

The great poems of *The Tower* and *The Winding Stair* are meditative monologues, the poet speaking to himself or to a friend. The
tone is intimate but dignified; the stanzas stately and slow moving
in their elaborate syntax; and they make few concessions to the

---

[1] Frederic Prokosch, 'Yeats's Testament', *The Spectator*, vol. 163 (4 August 1939),
p. 190. This and a selection of other reviews is to be found in Jon Stallworthy, ed., *Yeats:
Last Poems*, Casebook Series, 1968.

[2] 'The Great Yeats and the Latest', *Scrutiny*, viii (4 March 1940), pp. 437–40.

comprehension of readers unfamiliar with the poet's private world. A great proportion of the *Last Poems* are, by contrast, on public themes and addressed to the man in the street rather than the man in the drawing-room; hence the predominance of the ballad form; the simplified syntax and vocabulary, and the slackened tension of which Leavis speaks. One feels that Yeats is aware that his time is short and anxious to speak out—and be understood—while he can. This results in a certain number of very slight poems—successful though some may be in their own terms—but it also accounts for the driving force behind the best of the *Last Poems*. The flowing rhythm of 'Lapis Lazuli', uninterrupted by the more formal rhyming of such earlier stanza-paragraph poems as 'Mohini Chatterjee' and 'Easter 1916', is a principal source of its strength; as the swift lyrical openness of 'The Man and the Echo' and 'Under Ben Bulben' is appropriate to the self-questioning monologue of the death-bed and the Grand Testament.

IV

LADY, LOVER, AND CHAMBERMAID

•••

The Three Bushes

(AN INCIDENT FROM THE 'HISTORIA MEI TEMPORIS'
OF THE ABBÉ MICHEL DE BOURDEILLE)

  1. Said lady once to lover,
  2. 'None can rely upon
  3. A love that lacks its proper food;
  4. And if your love were gone
  5. How could you sing those songs of love?
  6. I should be blamed, young man.
  7.   *O my dear, O my dear.*

  8. 'Have no lit candles in your room,'
  9. That lovely lady said,
10. 'That I at midnight by the clock
11. May creep into your bed,
12. For if I saw myself creep in
13. I think I should drop dead.'
14.   *O my dear, O my dear.*

15. 'I love a man in secret,
16. Dear chambermaid,' said she.
17. 'I know that I must drop down dead
18. If he stop loving me,
19. Yet what could I but drop down dead
20. If I lost my chastity?
21.   *O my dear, O my dear.*

22. 'So you must lie beside him
23. And let him think me there,
24. And maybe we are all the same
25. Where no candles are,
26. And maybe we are all the same
27. That strip the body bare.'
28.   *O my dear, O my dear.*

29. But no dogs barked, and midnights chimed,
30. And through the chime she'd say,
31. 'That was a lucky thought of mine,
32. My lover looked so gay';
33. But heaved a sigh if the chambermaid
34. Looked half asleep all day.
35.   *O my dear, O my dear.*

36. 'No, not another song,' said he,
37. 'Because my lady came
38. A year ago for the first time
39. At midnight to my room,
40. And I must lie between the sheets
41. When the clock begins to chime.'
42.   *O my dear, O my dear.*

43. 'A laughing, crying, sacred song,
44. A leching song,' they said.
45. Did ever men hear such a song?
46. No, but that day they did.
47. Did ever man ride such a race?
48. No, not until he rode.
49.   *O my dear, O my dear.*

50. But when his horse had put its hoof
51. Into a rabbit-hole
52. He dropped upon his head and died.
53. His lady saw it all
54. And dropped and died thereon, for she
55. Loved him with her soul.
56.   *O my dear, O my dear.*

57. The chambermaid lived long, and took
58. Their graves into her charge,
59. And there two bushes planted
60. That when they had grown large
61. Seemed sprung from but a single root
62. So did their roses merge.
63.   *O my dear, O my dear.*

64. When she was old and dying,
65. The priest came where she was;
66. She made a full confession.
67. Long looked he in her face,
68. And O he was a good man
69. And understood her case.
70.   *O my dear, O my dear.*

71. He bade them take and bury her
72. Beside her lady's man,
73. And set a rose-tree on her grave,
74. And now none living can,
75. When they have plucked a rose there,
76. Know where its roots began.
77.   *O my dear, O my dear.*

The Lady's First Song

1. I turn round
2. Like a dumb beast in a show,
3. Neither know what I am
4. Nor where I go,
5. My language beaten
6. Into one name;
7. I am in love
8. And that is my shame.
9. What hurts the soul
10. My soul adores,
11. No better than a beast
12. Upon all fours.

The Lady's Second Song

1. What sort of man is coming
2. To lie between your feet?
3. What matter, we are but women.
4. Wash; make your body sweet;
5. I have cupboards of dried fragrance,
6. I can strew the sheet.
7.   *The Lord have mercy upon us.*

8. He shall love my soul as though
9. Body were not at all,
10. He shall love your body
11. Untroubled by the soul,
12. Love cram love's two divisions
13. Yet keep his substance whole.
14.   *The Lord have mercy upon us.*

15. Soul must learn a love that is
16. Proper to my breast,
17. Limbs a love in common
18. With every noble beast.
19. If soul may look and body touch,
20. Which is the more blest?
21.   *The Lord have mercy upon us.*

The Lady's Third Song

1. When you and my true lover meet
2. And he plays tunes between your feet,
3. Speak no evil of the soul,
4. Nor think that body is the whole,
5. For I that am his daylight lady
6. Know worse evil of the body;
7. But in honour split his love
8. Till either neither have enough,
9. That I may hear if we should kiss
10. A contrapuntal serpent hiss,
11. You, should hand explore a thigh,
12. All the labouring heavens sigh.

The Lover's Song

1. Bird sighs for the air,
2. Thought for I know not where,
3. For the womb the seed sighs.
4. Now sinks the same rest
5. On mind, on nest,
6. On straining thighs.

The Chambermaid's First Song

1. How came this ranger
2. Now sunk in rest,
3. Stranger with stranger,
4. On my cold breast?
5. What's left to sigh for?
6. Strange night has come;
7. God's love has hidden him
8. Out of all harm,
9. Pleasure has made him
10. Weak as a worm.

The Chambermaid's Second Song

1. From pleasure of the bed,
2. Dull as a worm,
3. His rod and its butting head
4. Limp as a worm,
5. His spirit that has fled
6. Blind as a worm.

The Spur

1. You think it horrible that lust and rage
2. Should dance attention upon my old age;
3. They were not such a plague when I was young;
4. What else have I to spur me into song?

THE prophetic voice of the *Last Poems* is counterpointed by that of the gleeman as, in *The Wanderings of Oisin and Other Poems*, Yeats's attempt at a saga in the grand manner had been balanced by such transcriptions from 'the book of the people' as 'Down by the Salley Gardens' and 'The Ballad of Moll Magee'. Despite his statements—especially in later life—to the contrary, it is clear that he wished to be both bard and *fili*; and, indeed, succeeded more than most poets of any century in speaking both to the many and the few.

Of all his ballads none is more justly famous than 'The Three Bushes'. Although several stages in the genesis of this and its attendant songs are revealed in *Letters on Poetry from W. B. Yeats to Dorothy Wellesley* and have been the subject of much critical discussion,[1] the manuscripts in the National Library of Ireland shed new light on the complex interrelation of poem with poem. Though some working drafts have almost certainly been lost, probably to Yeats's waste-paper basket, twenty-six manuscript and typescript sheets (or fragments of sheets) remain. I have numbered them F. 1 to F. 26 to avoid the inevitable confusion attendant upon having several folios with the one number discussed in the same essay. From these and the letters to Dorothy Wellesley can be plotted the progress of 'The Three Bushes', the Lady's three songs, 'The Lover's Song', the Chambermaid's two songs, and 'The Spur'.

Partridge follows T. R. Henn[2] in believing that the basic story of 'The Three Bushes' 'grew out of a ballad which Dorothy Wellesley was apparently working on when Yeats went to stay with her in June, 1936. While at Penns, he must have decided to write his own version of the story, perhaps in a kind of contest with his younger friend.' While this may have been what happened, I can find no

---

[1] Notably by Vivienne Koch in *W. B. Yeats / The Tragic Phase*, pp. 129–45; Edward B. Partridge in 'Yeats's "The Three Bushes"—Genesis and Structure', *Accent*, xvii. 2 (1957), pp. 67–80; and Arra M. Garab in 'Fabulous Artifice: Yeats's "Three Bushes" Sequence', *Criticism*, vii. 3 (1965), pp. 235–49. I am greatly indebted to these three critics.

[2] *The Lonely Tower*, second edition, 1965, p. 330.

evidence for it in the Yeats-Wellesley correspondence. The subject of 'The Three Bushes' is first mentioned by Yeats, who ends his letter of 22 June to Dorothy Wellesley: 'I add the chorus of my poem about the lady, the poet & the maid "O my dear, O my dear".[1] Yrs, W. B. Yeats.' Clearly they have discussed the topic, but the fact that he speaks of it as 'my poem' suggests that he regards the story as at least common property. His refrain he has taken from a Gaelic ballad, three verses of which he had 'put into English rhyme' and first published as an Appendix to his play *The Hour Glass* when it appeared in volume four of his *Collected Works in Verse and Prose* (1908). The ballad, which tells of a faithless wife, begins:

> I was going the road one day
> (O the brown and the yellow beer!)
> And I met with a man that was no right man
> (O my dear, O my dear).

It is a little difficult to pin-point the exact date on which Yeats began 'The Three Bushes'. On Tuesday 30 June he tells Dorothy Welles-ley that 'To-day I am content with life again—my work has gone well', and ends his letter: 'To-morrow I shall finish the play, then I write the ballad of lovers, the lady & the servant.' On Thursday 2 July, however, giving her 'the emotional diary' of his week, he writes:

> Next morning [Sunday 28 June] finish my play. Triumphant; believe I have written a masterpiece. That night, sleeping draft, artificially quieted, good sleep. Next morning [Monday 29 June] begin ballad about the poet the lady and the servant. Bad night. Next morning [Tuesday 30 June] finish ballad in the rough. Triumphant; believe I have written a masterpiece. Twelve verses, six lines each. Will take a whole Broadside. That afternoon—despair. . . . Then on Wednesday [1 July] I finish ballad in the smooth and decide to do no serious work for some days.

Since, when he wrote his earlier letter of 30 June, he was clearly not in the despair that overcame him during the afternoon, it seems probable that, having said he would write his ballad

---

[1] This was to become almost the refrain of Yeats's letters to Dorothy Wellesley. See *Letters on Poetry*, pp. 64, 80, 100, 111, and 113.

'to-morrow', he in fact finished that very morning a rough draft begun the previous day (though this was not admitted to Dorothy Wellesley).

The rough draft of 'The Three Bushes' that remains is too well advanced, I believe, for it to be the first. It does, however, show the poem in its original form of 'Twelve verses, six lines each'. 'The Rose Trees', its first title, may have been suggested by two of Dorothy Wellesley's poems, 'Thorn Tree' and 'Judas Tree', discussed some months earlier in their correspondence; and was presumably altered because Yeats had already written 'The Rose Tree', his powerful political ballad of the executed revolutionaries Pearse and Connolly. It is interesting to see the twin themes of love and death, inexplicably entwined in the rose symbol that Yeats inherited from Blake, appearing in the political ballad of 1920 and the narrative/philosophical ballad of 1936.

F. 1r begins the 'ballad in the rough' that would appear to have been drafted on the morning of Tuesday 30 June:[1]

three bushes
The ~~Rose Trees~~

I

'*Man's love that lacks its proper food*

None can rely upon

And could you sing no more of love

Your genius would be gone

And could that happen what were you

But a starving man

O my dear, O my dear

The lady recognizes that if the poet is denied love's 'proper food', he will have no substance for his songs.

---

[1] F. 1r–F. 4r are lined sheets from a loose-leaf notebook in which Yeats would seem to have written this draft; since, having crossed out stanza 7 on F. 3r, he wrote a correction on the facing F. 2v.

2

> *Light no candles in your room*
> '*Leave your chamber lights-unlit*'
>
> *That lovely lady said*
>   *I* (.) *when* ~~twelve~~ *twelve o'clock is sounding*
> ~~For at the stroke of midnight~~
>
> ~~I~~ *shall creep into your bed*
>   *if   saw   so*
> *But* ~~could~~ *I* ~~see~~ *myself* ~~so~~ *creep   in*
>
> *I think I should drop dead*
>
>   *O my dear O my dear*

That the invitation is for midnight is both a detail in the ballad tradition and one not without significance for Yeats, who frequently equated the moment of death with midnight; as in

> At stroke of midnight soul cannot endure
> A bodily or mental furniture.

In 'The Three Bushes' it is at midnight that the poet and chambermaid first make love—Yeats was of course aware of the sixteenth-century love/die conceit—and at midnight one year later that the poet literally meets his death.

3

> '*I love a man in secret*
>
> *Dear chamber maid*' *said she*
>   *must*
> '*I* ~~shou~~ *know that I* ~~shall~~ *drop down dead*
>
> *If he stop loving me*
>   ~~know~~   ~~dead if I~~
> ~~But think I must drop dead if I~~ ~~And drop down~~
>   ~~should lose~~
> ~~Do lose my chastity~~
>
>   *O my dear, O my dear*

Having cancelled lines 19 and 20, Yeats wrote a confident correction below this stanza:

> *Yet what could I but drop down dead*
>
> *If I lost my chastity*

before continuing on F. 2r:

4

>   *You*
> *So* ⎰ *must lie beside* ~~*him*~~ *him*
>   ⎱
>
> *And let him think me there*
>
> ⎡ *We are* | *may be* | *all the same*
> ⎣
>
> *Where no candles are*
>
> ⎡ *We are* | *may be* | *all the same*
> ⎣
>
> *When we our bodies bare*
>
>   *O my dear, O my dear*

The pun here on 'lie' (as in line 40, and line 2 of 'The Lady's Second Song') should not be overlooked. In two stanzas that were subsequently to be omitted the Lady soliloquizes further on the theme of 'A Last Confession':

5

>   ~~*And he*~~
>   *He*   *love my*
> ~~*He*~~ ⎰ *shall* ~~*my*~~ ⎰ *soul as though*
>   ⎱   ⎱
>
> *Body were not at all*
>   *He*
> ~~*And he*~~ *shall love your* ⟨ —.— ⟩ *body*
>
> *Untroubled by the soul*
>   *cram*   ~~*find*~~ *his*
> ~~*And love's*~~ *Love's* ~~*two divisions have his*~~ *two divisions*

~~Shall be complete~~   ~~And yet shall~~   *Yet keep his substance whole*

Yet shall love be whole

O my dear O my dear

6

Soul
~~My soul soul~~
~~And I~~ *must learn a love that* ~~is~~

Is   Proper to my breast
                              A
~~Your~~ *limbs* ~~must learn this love~~ *love in common*

With every noble beast
~~must~~ *may*
If soul ~~can~~ *look & body* ~~touch~~ *touch*
        is the more
Which ~~can be more~~ *blessed*

O my dear O my dear

With the dramatist's skilful use of direct speech Yeats is able to dispense with linking narrative and advance, on F. 3*r*, to the poet a year later being pressed by his drinking companions for another song.

7

'*Another song*' '*O no said he,*
A ~~song, a song another~~ *song*
        My ~~dear love first came~~ *My darling poppet came*
~~'No not one song said he~~
                    ~~on the stroke of~~ *the clock strikes*
'*A year* ~~ago~~ *ago* ~~when midnight strikes struck~~ *this very night*
        At midnight into my room
~~My love came first to~~ *me*
        And I must lie between the sheets
~~And if I (.) spurs I may~~
                When it begins to boom,
Hear that in her company'

O my dear, O my dear

In this stanza, which Yeats cancelled with diagonal strokes of his pen, there should be noted the momentary appearance of the lover's spurs; since the poem 'The Spur' can, I believe, be traced back to these. Stanza 7 is revised on F. 2*v*:

G

I say (. . .) no
'Another song ~~but~~ no said he

~~My~~ Because my lady came

A year ago for the first time

At midnight to my room

And I must lie between the sheets

When ~~the~~ bell begins to boom

     O my dear, O my dear

The poem continues on F. 3*r*:

8

          sacred
'A ~~holy~~, laughing, ~~song~~ sighing | song'

A letching song' said they
      hear
Did ever man ~~sing~~ such a song
  not
No | before that day

Did ever man ride such a race

Not till he rode away

     O my dear, O my dear

9

 when   *had put its hoof*
But ~~O his~~ horse it ~~stum~~ stamped
 Into
~~At~~ a rabbit hole
 dropped
He ~~fell~~ upon his head & died;
  that
His lady saw it all
     ~~down~~   *there so*
~~And she too~~ dropped & died ~~because there there so~~ for she

(.) Loved him with her soul

    (.) O my dear, O my dear

10

F. 4r: The chamber maid lived on ~~&~~ *and* took

Their graves into her charge

Then there two bushes planted

That when they had grown large

~~Seem~~ Seemed sprung from | *out* a single root

So did their roses merge

O my dear, O my dear

11

When she was old & dying

The priest came where she was

She made a full confession;
~~He looked her~~ *Long looked he* in ~~the~~ *her* face,

And O he was a good man

And understood her case.

O my dear, O my dear

12

He bade them take & bury her

Beside her ladies man

And set a rose tree on her grave

And now none ~~live~~ living can

When they have plucked a rose there

No where its roots have run

O my dear, O my dear

On F. 5*r*, a typescript heavily corrected in ink, Yeats attempts a radical revision of stanza 1:

And I must bring the bread & meat
Before your love is gone

~~*And all those love songs finished*~~
~~*And I to blame young man*~~
For did you rhyme no more of love
~~*I should be blamed young man*~~
I were to blame young man

The Ballad of
| THE THREE BUSHES
∧

~~Passion~~ *Love that is starved of*
'~~Man's love that lacks its~~ proper food

None can rely upon
   And I must spread the table or
~~And could you sing no more of love~~
      ~~passion will~~
Your ~~genius would~~ be gone
   You if that ~~should~~ *happen*
~~And could that happen what were you~~
   Were but
~~But a starving man~~'

         O my dear, O my dear.

~~would rhyme~~ *of love*
~~would sing no more~~
And you ~~could you not~~
No more make songs of love
~~sing of love~~
~~Would drop down dead young man~~
And I be blamed young man

'*So light*   ~~*But light*~~   ~~*Blow out the*~~
      "~~Light no~~ | *candles in your* ~~room~~"
      The ∧
      ~~That~~ *lovely lady said*
That   ~~*And*~~ *I at midnight by the clock*
      "~~I when twelve o'clock is sounding~~
May   ~~*Shall*~~
      ~~Shall~~ | *creep into your bed*
      ∧
      But if I saw myself creep in

"~~Leave no lit candles in your room~~"

I think I should drop dead"

<u>O my dear, O my dear.</u>

"I love a man in secret

Dear chambermaid," said she

'I know that I must drop down dead

If he stop loving me

Yet what could I but drop down dead

If I lost my chastity?

<u>O my dear, O my dear.</u>

F. 6r is a three-inch strip of typing paper containing a typed version of stanza 4 identical with that Yeats sent Dorothy Wellesley with his undated letter of [A] Tuesday [in July 1936].[1] In this, line 27, 'When the body's bare', is a considerable improvement on the contorted 'When we our bodies bare' of the manuscript; and is further tautened by the change to 'That strip the body['s] bare':

"So you must lie beside him

And let him think me there
And
⎰Maybe we are all the same
⋏   *lit*
Where no⎰candles are
  And maybe
~~Maybe~~ we are all the same
  That strip
~~When~~⎰ the body's bare"
   ⋏

<u>O my dear, O my dear.</u>

I suspect that F. 6r originally included typescript versions of stanzas 5 and 6 of the manuscript, but that these were torn off because such an extension of the Lady's philosophical soliloquy

---

[1] *Letters on Poetry*, pp. 73–7.

slowed up the narrative and was, in dramatic terms, out of place. On the typescript F. 7r Yeats is still wrestling unsuccessfully with lines 36–41:

> "No, not another song" said he
>   '*And I must hurry home*
>   ~~Because my lady came~~   *and a day ago*
> *For*   *Twelve months & ~~a day ago~~* (. . . .)
>   ~~A year ago for the first time~~
> *She came*   ~~*The first time my lady*~~ *came & she will come*
>   ~~At midnight to my room~~
>   ~~*must*~~ *If I lie still*
>   ~~And I must lie~~ between the sheets
>   *And The clock will*   *Midnight's on the ~~str~~ chime*
>   ~~When bells begins to boom~~"   *~~the great bells~~ chime*
>
>   <u>O my dear,</u> <u>O my dear.</u>

Once again we see him attempting to rewrite a stanza which, with the exception of line 41, was to find its way into the finished text of the poem.

>   *sighing*
> "A laughing, ~~crying,~~ sacred song
>
> A letching song" | said | they |
>
> Did ever man hear such a song?
>   *No, no man ever did*
> ~~No not before that~~ day
>
> Did ever man ride such a race
>   No not until he rode
> Not ~~till he rode~~ away.
>
>   <u>O my dear,</u> <u>O my dear.</u>
>
> But when his horse had put its hoof
>
> Into a rabbit hole
>
> He dropped upon his head and died
>
> His lady ~~that~~ saw it all;

> *His lady dropped & died*
> ~~Dropped and died thereon~~ for she
> *Had loved*
> ~~Loved~~ him with her soul.

> O my dear, O my dear.

Dying, the lady fulfils her earlier prophecy:

> 'I know that I must drop down dead

> If he stop loving me . . .'

Dissatisfied with his corrections to lines 38–41, Yeats turned this page on its side and wrote along the left-hand margin:

> *I seek a certain room*

> *For twelve months & a day ago*

> *My lady came for the first time*
> *And*
> ~~*For*~~ *I must hurry home*

There remains no typescript version of lines 29–35 or 57–77; but, before considering the changes that took place before the poem's first appearance in print, it is necessary to return to Yeats's letter of 2 July. This at first ended: 'I am longing to read your ballad. I will not send you mine until yours is finished. Yours with love and affection, W. B. Yeats.' He then added a postscript, 'Just come',[1] and continued: 'Here you have a masterpiece. (I have just put in the rhymes to make it a ballad.)' With that disconcerting lack of critical judgement sometimes found in his assessment of the work of other poets, he praised Dorothy Wellesley's stilted pseudo-archaic stanzas as 'far better than my laboured livelier verses'. On 10 July he wrote to her again, suggesting further changes, and on 14 July she replied: 'I send the revised version of the Ballad. . . . May I have yours now? I long to see it.' This he sent with a letter dated 'Tuesday' (probably 14 July), in which he wrote: 'I now like my long Ballad of the Three Bushes again. I have written two other poems on the same theme.'

---

[1] Dorothy Wellesley's own words were published in the Cuala Press *Broadsides*, 1937, first incorrectly, with three final verses which were cut out because of Yeats's criticism, and then correctly on an erratum slip.

That his ballad is again in favour suggests that he has improved it,
and certainly there were a number of significant changes made
before its first appearance in print. The manuscript revisions to the
typescript of stanza 1 were abandoned; two of the characters introduced in line 1; and lines 2–6 so reshaped that the stressed word
'love', echoing 'lover', is repeated three times:

> Line 1. Said lady once to lover
>   2. 'None can rely upon
>   3. A love that lacks its proper food;
>   4. And if your love were gone
>   5. How could you sing those songs of love?
>   6. I should be blamed, young man.
>   8. 'Leave no lit candles . . .' *becomes* 'Have no lit candles . . .'

The fact that lines 29–35 appear neither in the manuscript nor typescript drafts suggests that they may have been added when the
original stanzas 5 and 6 were cut out. F. 8 is a leaf from *The London
Mercury* (January 1937, pages 265–6) on which 'The Three Bushes'
made its first printed appearance. The new stanza 5—with its
anticipation of the line from the poem 'To Dorothy Wellesley',
'For now the horizon's bought strange dogs are still'[1]—Yeats has
corrected in ink on F. 8r:

> *But no dogs barked*
>   ~~And dogs were still~~
> Line 29. ~~Dogs did not bark~~ And no dogs barked though midnights
>   chimed;
>   30.   And at night time she would say,
>   31.   "That was a lucky thought of mine
>   32.   My lover looks so gay~~:~~"   ; /
>   33.   But heaved a sigh if the chambermaid
>   34.   Looked half asleep all day.
>   35.   O my dear, O my dear.

Line 32 echoes the key word of 'Lapis Lazuli', an epithet that Yeats
applies to himself in his letter of 5 September to Dorothy Wellesley:
'Then I can fold my hands and be a wise old man and gay.'

The pre-publication changes to the remaining stanzas were less
important. As with stanza 1 he rejected his manuscript revisions to
the typescript stanza 6, altering only the following lines:

---

[1] For an explanation of this line see *Letters on Poetry*, p. 53.

Line 41. When the bells begin to boom
        became
        When the clock begins to chime

   43. . . . sighing . . . *became* . . . crying . . .

   46. No, no man ever did
        became
        No, but that day they did.

54–5. His lady dropped & died for she
        Had loved him with her soul.
        became
        And dropped and died thereon, for she
        Loved him with her soul.

   57. . . . lived on . . . *became* . . . lived long . . .

   61. . . . from out . . . *became* . . . from but . . .

   76. No where its roots have run
        became
        Know where its roots began.

There were two further changes (apart from punctuation) for the poem's second appearance, in *A Broadside*, No. 3 (New Series), March 1937:

Line 29. And no dogs barked though midnights chimed,
        became
        But no dogs barked and midnights chimed

Finally, three more lines were altered for its first printing in book form—*New Poems*, 1938:

Line 25. . . . no lit candles . . . *became* . . . no candles . . .

   30. And at night time would she say,
        became
        And through the chime she'd say,

   32. . . . lover looks . . . *became* . . . lover looked . . .

On 14 or 17 September Yeats had written to Dorothy Wellesley: 'When we meet we will decide upon the name of the fourteenth or fifteenth[1] fabulist who made the original story'; and wrote by way of postscript to his letter of 15 November: 'I am describing *The Three Bushes* as "founded upon an incident from the *Historia mei Temporis* of the Abbé Michel de Bourdeilie" '. Garab comments that

> no one has been able to trace either the 'fabulist' or his book. For good reason, perhaps, not only because 'Bourdeille' is a pun on *bordel* ('brothel') as Miss Koch (p. 131) has indicated, but also because *bourde* means 'fib', 'humbug'. On the other hand, Yeats may have known of Pierre de Bourdeille, abbé et seigneur de Brantôme (ca. 1540–1614), a *bon vivant* who, after suffering a severe fall from a horse (see details of Yeats's poem . . .), chronicled often fancifully and usually frankly the lives of numerous interesting personages.[2]

In this connection it should be remembered how Yeats had earlier disguised the author of *A Vision* in a beard, fancy dress, and the alias of Giraldus.

One feature of 'The Three Bushes' has an interesting parallel in 'Proud Costello, MacDermot's Daughter, and the Bitter Tongue', a story from *The Secret Rose* (1897). This ends with Costello swimming out into the lake in answer to a ghostly summons from his dead sweetheart Oona MacDermot:

> and when he had gone a little way he sank without a struggle, like a man passing into sleep and dreams.
>
> The next day a poor fisherman found him among the reeds upon the lake shore, lying upon the white lake sand with his arms flung out as though he lay upon a rood, and carried him to his own house. And the very poor lamented over him and sang the keen, and when the time had come, laid him in the Abbey on Insula Trinitatis with only the ruined altar between him and Oona the daughter of Dermott, and planted above them two ash-trees that in after days wove their branches together and mingled their trembling leaves.

2

It is time now to turn back to Yeats's statement of 14 July that 'I have written two other poems on the same theme.' The first of these was 'The Lady's Second Song', into which went the two stanzas

---

[1] I think it almost certain that Yeats unintentionally omitted the word 'century'.
[2] Op. cit., p. 238.

jettisoned from 'The Three Bushes'. In faint—now almost illegible
—pencil, stanza 1 of his new poem takes shape on F. 1v:

> All our work is one work
> Here ~~for our work is but our~~ work
>   Wash—
> ~~When you~~ make your body sweet
>   have cupboards of dried oranges
> I ~~shall (.) fragrant herbs~~
>
> ~~And strew~~ And I shall strew the sheet
>
> ~~To strew upon the sheet~~
>
>   ~~May God have mercy~~
>
> ~~For he shall love my soul as though~~
>
> ~~What manner~~
>
>
> What manner of man is coming
>
> To lie between your feet
>   ~~O~~
>   God have mercy God have
>   mercy

With the same pencil Yeats sketched out 'The Lady's Third Song',
as it was later to be entitled, on F. 9r:

> The Lady to the Chambermaid
>
> Should you with   ~~true~~
> ~~When you~~ & my ~~old~~ lover meet
>
> And he plays tunes between your feet
>   Remember body is not the whole
>
> ~~Do not dare abuse the soul~~ abuse the soul
>
> ~~How can body be the whole~~   think it (.)
>
> Should it dare abuse the soul
>
>
> ~~Should you dare his daylight~~
>   that
> I am his daylight lady

Will in love abuse the body

Must in love abuse the body

Sware that will never stray

From either neither night day

I must hear if we dare kiss
      when I (.   )
That I may hear if we kiss
      That Hear or music of the serpent's hiss
The music of the serpent's hiss

You when he has wound your thigh

All the labouring heavens sigh

The antithesis of 'daylight lady' and night/chambermaid, more pointed here than in the finished poem, is reminiscent of 'Chosen';[1] while the Lady's euphemistic and literary serpent image, continuing into the line 'You when he has wound your thigh' prefigures the gross but fitting worm of the Chambermaid's Songs.

On F. 4v Yeats redrafts 'The Lady's Third Song':

When you & my true lover meet
When you with I your lover meet

And he plays tunes between your feet

Remember body is not the soul whole

If you dare abuse the soul
  must that am
I shall be his daylight lady

Outrageously abuse the body

But swear that he will never stray

For either neither night & day

[1] For the drafts of this poem see *Between the Lines*, Chapter VII.

> *hear if we should kiss*
> *That I may* (.) *I* (.) ~~*her kiss*~~
> *That contrapuntal serpent*
> ~~*Hear music of the serpent*~~ *hiss*
>
> ~~*You when hand touch your thigh*~~
>
> ~~*Hear*~~ *All the labouring heavens sigh*

Under this he wrote a correction to line 11:

> *You should hand explore a thigh*

Partridge suggests that Yeats may have picked up the daring phrase 'either neither' from 'The Phoenix and the Turtle',[1] Dorothy Wellesley's favourite poem:[2]

> Reason, in itself confounded,
> Saw division grow together,
> To themselves yet either neither,
> Simple were so well compounded.

In his discussion of what he well describes as a 'latently passionate friendship between an attractive woman and a vehement old man', Partridge calls attention to Yeats's letter of 21 July explaining his revisions of Dorothy Wellesley's ballad, which ends with a revealing passage: 'Ah my dear how it added to my excitement when I re-made that poem of yours to know it was your poem. I re-made you and myself into a single being. We triumphed over each other and I thought of *The Turtle and the Phoenix.*'

The first of the two typescripts of 'The Lady's Second Song', F. 10*r*, illustrates clearly the manner of the poem's composition; the second and third stanzas have been cut out of a typescript of 'The Three Bushes' and pasted on to another quarto sheet of typing paper under a much improved stanza 1:

The Lady to her Chambermaid

I

What manner of man is coming

To lie between your feet

---

[1] Op. cit., p. 76.
[2] See *Letters on Poetry*, p. 150.

~~wer~~ we're
What matter ~~we are~~ but two women   ;

Wash ~~and,~~ make your body sweet   ;

I have cupboards of dried fragrance

I can strew the sheet.
            The Lord have mercy on us
            ~~May God have mercy, God have mercy.~~

"He shall love my soul~~d~~ as though

Bod~~a~~y were not at all

He shall love your body

Untroubled by the soul

Love cram his two divisions

Yet keep his substance whole
            The Lord have mercy on us
            ~~O my dear, O my dear.~~

"Soul must learn a love that is

Proper to my breast

Limbs ~~must learn~~ a love in common

With every noble beast

If soul may look and body touch

Which is the more blest?"

~~O my dear, O my dear.~~
The Lord have mercy on us

There can be no doubt, I think, that the two philosophical stanzas from 'The Three Bushes' fit the new poem better than the narrative ballad. Not that one should overlook the dramatic element in 'The Lady's Second Song'. This begins in mid-conversation; the

Chambermaid having asked what she may expect. The Lady, pondering her reply, repeats the question:

> What manner of man is coming
>
> To lie between your feet

only to dismiss it with her next breath:

> *~~per~~ we're*
> What matter ~~we are~~ but two women;

Then follows a practical instruction:

> Wash, make your body sweet;

Lines 5 and 6 perhaps contain an echo of Shakespeare's Queen Gertrude speaking over Ophelia's grave:

> Sweets to the sweet: farewell!
> I hoped thou shouldst have been my Hamlet's wife;
> I thought thy bride-bed to have deckt, sweet maid,
> And not have strew'd thy grave.

Partridge says of the contrapuntal structure of these poems that

> Sometimes the lines express the counterpoint directly, as in 'A laughing, crying, sacred song,/A letching song'; sometimes, only indirectly, as in the Lady's words—'I can strew the sheet'—which evoke the image of the Lady taking the part of her maid in preparing the marriage bed, even as the maid is going to take her part in being the bride.

When Yeats sent the Lady's Second and Third Song to Dorothy Wellesley, they appeared as parts I and II of the one poem entitled 'The Lady to her Chambermaid' and their lines were set out in pairs (except for the indented and isolated refrain 'The Lord have mercy upon us'). Four lines were altered:

Line 3. . . . we're but two women;
> *became*
> . . . we are but women;

5–6. I have cupboards of dried fragrance
I can strew the sheet

became

I shall find a perfume
To scatter on the sheet

9. Body were not at all

became

Body were not all

A second typescript, F. 11*r*, has its title 'The Lady to her Chamber-maid' corrected to 'The Lady's Second Song'; the figure I is deleted, indicating that Yeats now saw it as a separate Song; and the text, except for one word and minor differences of punctuation, is that first printed. The earlier readings of lines 5, 6, and 9 have been restored.

Line 12. . . . his two divisions *becomes* . . . love's two divisions

13. Yet keeps . . . *becomes* Yet keep . . .

Before the poem's first publication in *New Poems* (1938), 'What manner of man' in line 1 was changed to 'What sort of man', pre-sumably to avoid the jingle of manner, man, matter. At this point a misprint—'breast' for 'beast'—crept into line 18, but this was cor-rected in *Last Poems and Plays* (1940).

F. 12*r* contains a manuscript fair-copy of 'The Lady's Third Song' (at this stage entitled 'Lady to Chambermaid') that differs only in punctuation from the finished text. The rough draft has been considerably tightened:

Lines 3–8:   *Remember body is not the* ~~*soul*~~ *whole*

If you dare abuse the soul
must that am
I ~~*shall be*~~ *his daylight lady*

Outrageously abuse the body

But swear that he will never stray

For either neither night & day

have become

> *Speak no evil of the soul,*
>   *the*
> *Nor think that body is* | *whole,*
>   Λ
>
> *For I, that am his daylight lady,*
>
> *Know worse evil of the body,*
>
> *But in honour ~~slip~~ split his love*
>   *Till*
> *~~That~~ either neither have enough;*

Line 10.   That contrapuntal . . . *has become* A contrapuntal . . .

Yeats presumably introduced the less obtrusive indefinite article in line 10 because the demonstrative 'That' clashed with the same word at the start of the previous line. The one typescript of this poem, F. 13*r*, has no punctuation but a final full stop; the figure II has been crossed out in pencil and replaced by 'The Lady's Third Song'.

Under the fair-copy of this poem on F. 12*r* is a rough draft, as yet untitled, of 'The Spur':

> *Why do you think it ~~strange~~ odd*
>   *~~lady~~   if that*
> *~~Do not reproach me, lady,~~ for Lust & ~~Rage~~ Rage*
>
> *~~D~~*
>
> *Should dance attendance upon my old age?*
>   *That*
> *~~They did not plague me so when I was young~~*
>
> *~~What else have I to spur me into song~~*
>   *~~They were~~*
> *They were not such a plague when I was young*
>
> *What else have I to spur me into song?*

The lady, who appears in no other draft of this poem, must be Dorothy Wellesley to whom Yeats sent a more finished version some five months later. Having ended his letter to her of 4 December, 'Forgive all this ['infuriated comment' on the alleged forgery of the Casement diaries] my dear but I have told you that my poetry all comes from rage or lust', he began his letter of 9 December:

My dear Dorothy,
   Here is my final apology

> You think it horrible that Lust and Rage
> Should dance attendance upon my old age.
> They were not such a plague when I was young.
> What else have I to spur me into song?

There are two typescripts of this quatrain (F. 14*r* and F. 15*r*), one entitled 'What other Spur'[1] and the other 'The Spur', that differ in nothing but punctuation from the version first printed in *The London Mercury* (March 1938). At its second printing 'dance attendance' in line 2 was changed to 'dance attention', but I share the view of G. D. P. Allt and others that the earlier reading is the better.

On 9 November Yeats had sent Dorothy Wellesley an untitled version of 'The Lover's Song', which he said came 'this morning':

> Bird sighs for the air,
>
> Thought for I know not where,
>
> For the womb the seed sighs.
>
> Sinks the same rest
>
> On intellect, on nest,
>
> On straining thighs?

And on 15 November he wrote:

That poem that begins 'Bird sighs for the air' is now one of the poems attendant on 'The Three Bushes'. It is 'The Lovers Song'. I follow it with 'The Chamber Maid's prayer before Dawn' & 'The Chambermaid's song after his death'. Here they are [texts follow.]

---

[1] A pencilled (but late?) draft of the poem, with this title and in this form, appears with 'The Great Day', 'Parnell', and 'What was Lost' on a sheet of notepaper headed 'Riversdale, Willbrook, Rathfarnham, Dublin'.

What I take to be the earliest remaining draft of 'The Lover's Song'
is written along the right-hand margin of F. 16r:

Lover's Song

Bird ~~sighs~~ sighs for the air,

Thought for I know not where

For the womb the seed sighs

Now sinks the same rest

On the mind, on the nest,
        straining
On the ~~straining~~ thighs.

Before this, however, Yeats had written down the page:

Lady Songs

   ⟨ . ⟩
I turn ~~around~~

Like a dumb beast in a show

~~In a s~~ Neither know what I am

Nor where I go

    my
~~All~~ ⌐language beaten
    ∧
Into one name,

~~Because~~ I am in love

And that~~s~~ my shame   *is/*

What most hurts ~~the~~ soul   *the/*

~~I most~~

My soul most adores

No better than a beast

Upon all fours

Chambermaid forgets before dawn

Whence came this ranger

Sunk into rest

Stranger with stranger

On my cold breast

The still night hide him

Out of all harm

Now pleasure has made

Weak as a worm

Chambermaid ~~after his death~~ *sums up*

From pleasure of the bed

Weak as a worm

His rod & its butting head

Limp as a worm

~~*A*~~ *(.) shaddow* ~~am~~ *among the dead*

Thin as a worm

A spirit that has fled

Bare as a worm

It is difficult to see in what order these four songs were written. The version of 'The Lover's Song' sent to Dorothy Wellesley on 9 November has a line 5

On intellect, on nest,

apparently further from its final form

On mind, on nest,

than that on F. 16r. This folio, however, has an early version of 'The Lady's First Song', a poem that Yeats does not send Dorothy

Wellesley until 20 November; an earlier version of 'The Chamber-maid's First Song' than that in his letter of 15 November; but a later version of 'The Chambermaid's Second Song' than the one in that letter. To avoid confusion, I am assuming that 'The Lover's Song' was written first; then 'The Lady's First Song'; and then the Chambermaid's two Songs.

There is one further manuscript version of 'The Lover's Song', unpunctuated but for one comma and a final full stop, on F. 17r.

It ends:

> *Now sinks the same rest*
>
> *On intellect, on nest*
>
> *On straining thighs.*

The changes to line 5 take place on two typescripts corrected in ink. 'Mind' replaces 'intellect' on F. 18r:

mind, | on | On ~~intellect, on~~ nest   ~~upon~~
the mind, on the   ~~The mind | the | upon~~

and the line is finally trimmed on F. 19r:

On | ~~The~~ mind, on ~~the~~ nest

The finished poem has what Garab, in his excellent analysis, calls

a rising and falling movement characteristic of the course of love's energy. This pattern of desire, suspension, and rest is expressed in the *aabccb* rhyme scheme: after *aa* we get *b*, and expecting *b* again, we get instead suspense, *c*, doubled in the fifth line until resolution, *b*, is achieved at last.[1]

The version of 'The Lady's First Song' sent to Dorothy Wellesley on 20 November has four lines significantly different from that on F. 16r:

Line 3. I know not what I am

    5. And all my words are beaten

    9. That which most hurts the soul

   10. My soul adores

[1] Op. cit., p. 244.

These appear in the two typescripts (F. 20*r* and F. 21*r*) as:

Line 3. Neither know what I am

    5. My language beaten

    9. What ~~most~~ hurts the soul

    10. My soul adores,

This compression makes it a tighter, better balanced poem; the stressed repetition of 'beast' and 'soul' fitting it for its function as link between the ballad and the subsequent songs.

The version of 'The Chambermaid's First Song' (then entitled 'The Chambermaid's prayer before Dawn') sent to Dorothy Wellesley on 15 November is sufficiently different from that on F. 16*r* to warrant quotation in full:

I

Whence came this ranger

Now sunk into rest,

Stranger with stranger,

On my cold breast?

What's left to sigh for

Now all are the same?

What would he die for

Before night came?

May God's love hide him

Out of all harm,

Now pleasure has made him

Weak as a worm.

The poem has been extended by four lines. The introduction of 'sigh' picks up a word found also in 'The Three Bushes', 'The

Lady's Third Song', and 'The Lover's Song'; as the line 'Now all
are the same' echoes the Lady's reflection in 'The Three Bushes':

> And maybe we are all the same
> That strip the body bare.

Whereas in the earlier draft 'still night hides' the Lover, the
Chambermaid now prays that 'God's love' may 'hide him Out of
all harm'. She, we remember, on her deathbed was to make a full
confession to the priest who 'understood her case' and presumably
granted her absolution.

On 28 November Yeats wrote:

I have changed the adjective in the worm poem

> Whence came this ranger
>
> Sunk into rest
>
> Stranger with stranger
>
> On my cold breast?
>
> May God's love hide him
>
> Out of all harm
>
> When pleasure has made him
>
> Dull as a worm.

It is curious that he should mention the change of adjective—'weak'
to 'dull'—but not the fact that he has cut out four lines to make it
the same length as 'The Chambermaid's Second Song'. The manuscript draft that appears below 'The Lover's Song' on F. 17r is
headed 'The Chambermaid's Song' and is the same as the twelve-
line version sent to Dorothy Wellesley on 15 November, except for
two lines altered to their final form:

Line 1. Whence came . . . *has become* How came . . .

    2. . . . into rest, *has become* . . . in rest

and one other change:

    5*a* Now all . . . *has become* Where all . . .

In the last line 'dull' has reverted to 'weak'. F. 22*r*, the first of two typescripts, is identical to the manuscript version on F. 17*r*, except for punctuation; but F. 23*r*, the second typescript, marks a considerable advance. The title appears for the first time; lines 5*a* and *b* have been jettisoned; and line 6 is corrected in ink:

    Strange   ~~Before~~ night │ came   │*has o*/

The poem being now a Song rather than a 'prayer before Dawn', Yeats made one final change before publication:

    Line 7. May God's love hide him

        became

        God's love has hidden him

The earliest form of 'The Chambermaid's Second Song' appears to be that in the letter to Dorothy Wellesley of 15 November:

II

Joy laid him on my bed

Weak as a worm,

His rod, that rose up unfed,

Limp as a worm.

A shadow has gone to the dead

Thin as a worm,

Where can his spirit have fled

Bare as a worm?

On 20 November he sent her a revised version incorporating the following changes:

    Line 1. Joy laid him on my bed

        becomes

        Joy left him upon my bed

3. His rod, that rose up unfed,

   becomes

   His rod & its butting head

He added that he 'wrote the poem in this letter for the sake of the second line (wrongly expressed in the version I sent you two days ago, "unfed" being clearly the reverse of true)'. To this Dorothy Wellesley replied on 25 November:

> Am much amused about the worm-poem. Of course it struck me instantly, and I think therefore that Higgins is right. Otherwise there are lovely things my dear; but like all women I dislike worms. . . . Can you think of something to take the place of the worms? Worms we are and unto worms shall we return.

The one manuscript draft, F. 24*r*, introduces a new first line that echoes line 9 of the previous song:

   From pleasure of the bed,

Line 4*a*. A shadow has gone to the dead

   has become

   His shaddow among the dead

and in the last line 'Bare' has become, more appropriately, 'Blind'. On 28 November Yeats sent Dorothy Wellesley a version the same as that on F. 24*r*, except that line 4*a* is now 'A shadow among the dew', and 'Blind' in the last line has been temporarily replaced by 'Bare'. This version is followed by an answer to Dorothy Wellesley's criticisms: 'The "worm" is right, its repulsiveness is right—so are the adjectives—"dull", "limp", "thin", "bare", all suggested by the naked body of the man, & taken with the worm by that body abject & helpless. All suggest her detachment, her "cold breast", her motherlike prayer.' The two typescripts of this poem (F. 25*r* and F. 26*r*) are, except for punctuation, the same as the printed text; though the former shows Yeats reinstating, in ink, the lines he ultimately cancelled:

   His shadow among the dead

   Weak as a worm,

The finished poem is, as Partridge says,

within itself contrapuntal, each of the worm similes counterpointing the
line directly before and the line directly after, and the last returning, in
the endless cycle of death, birth, pleasure, death, to the first line again.
The worm, the traditional symbol of death, is associated here with sleep-
ing man, limp phallus, fleeing spirit, and dead body. Man turns into
worm because of love, because of death. The death begins in the midst
of love: strange night has come, partly because two strangers meet in a
wordless embrace, partly because such a night is the emblem of the death
that awaits to embrace us all. [1]

So the worm in the bed of 'The Chambermaid's Second Song'
counterpoints the worm in the grave of 'The Three Bushes' and
the cycle's end returns to its beginning. Though one can fairly say
of the finished ballad and its attendant songs, that

> now none living can
> When they have plucked a rose there
> Know where its roots began

the manuscripts reveal something of the subterranean development
of these poems and enable us to appreciate more fully their complex
harmonies.

The measure of their intricacy can perhaps best be seen by a comparison with the original forms of such early ballads as those of
Father O'Hart and Moll Magee. Despite the leavening of Irish
words (*shoneen*, *sleiveens*, *boreen*) requiring an academic gloss indicative of a more intimate acquaintance with the language of the people
than he possessed, despite the place-names and the colloquialisms,
these ballads seem to owe more to Wordsworth's *Lyrical Ballads*
than to the tradition of folk poetry that Yeats was trying to revive.
Their literary descent is betrayed by an abundance of adjectives,
many of them succeeding their nouns, and a lack of narrative
momentum. No genuine folk ballad would contain such a syntactic
contortion as

> All loved him, only the *shoneen*,

[1] Op. cit., p. 78.

('only' meaning 'except') or would end with a didactic interjection
by the balladeer:

> This way were all reproved,
> Who dig old customs up.

'The Ballad of Father O'Hart' and 'The Ballad of Moll Magee'
each contain more adjectives than 'The Three Bushes' (which has
77 lines to their 40 and 56), and in the later poem an adjective is
never used to pad out a line but only to supply necessary information: 'proper food', 'lit candles', 'lovely lady', and so on. Whereas
the narrative skeletons of the early ballads are slight and support a
good deal of descriptive fat, 'The Three Bushes' and its attendant
songs are all narrative bone and intellectual muscle. Story and
allegory advance in perfect step. The language is spare and simple
without archaisms or inversions, the direct speech truly colloquial
and in character, and stanza by stanza the meditative refrain slows
down the pace of the narrative, ringing its ironic changes. '*O my dear,
O my dear*' is spoken in turn by lady to lover (twice), lady to chambermaid, lady to chambermaid and lover, chambermaid to lover, lover
to lady (twice), lady to lover again, chambermaid over the graves of
lady and lover, and priest to chambermaid (twice). At the same time
one is justified, I believe, in hearing '*O my dear, O my dear*' as
Yeats's aside to Dorothy Wellesley. This sophisticated use of refrain
is one of the most immediately noticeable differences between
Yeats's early ballads and those of the *Last Poems*. The ultimate
triumph of 'The Three Bushes', however, remains its union of the
popular and the intellectual. It is sung, for its racy narrative, in the
streets of Dublin by many who have no inkling of the philosophical
argument that occupies the few.

> How can they know
> Truth flourishes where the student's lamp has shone,
> And there alone, that have no solitude?

LONG-LEGGED FLY AND THE STATUES

Long-legged Fly

1. That civilization may not sink,
2. Its great battle lost,
3. Quiet the dog, tether the pony
4. To a distant post;
5. Our master Caesar is in the tent
6. Where the maps are spread,
7. His eyes fixed upon nothing,
8. A hand under his head.
9. *Like a long-legged fly upon the stream*
10. *His mind moves upon silence.*

11. That the topless towers be burnt
12. And men recall that face,
13. Move most gently if move you must
14. In this lonely place.
15. She thinks, part woman, three parts a child,
16. That nobody looks; her feet
17. Practice a tinker shuffle
18. Picked up on a street.
19. *Like a long-legged fly upon the stream*
20. *Her mind moves upon silence.*

21. That girls at puberty may find
22. The first Adam in their thought,
23. Shut the door of the Pope's chapel,
24. Keep those children out.
25. There on that scaffolding reclines
26. Michael Angelo.
27. With no more sound than the mice make
28. His hand moves to and fro.
29. *Like a long-legged fly upon the stream*
30. *His mind moves upon silence.*

The Statues

1. Pythagoras planned it. Why did the people stare?
2. His numbers, though they moved or seemed to move
3. In marble or in bronze, lacked character.
4. But boys and girls, pale from the imagined love
5. Of solitary beds, knew what they were,
6. That passion could bring character enough,
7. And pressed at midnight in some public place
8. Live lips upon a plummet-measured face.

9. No! Greater than Pythagoras, for the men
10. That with a mallet or a chisel modelled these
11. Calculations that look but casual flesh, put down
12. All Asiatic vague immensities,
13. And not the banks of oars that swam upon
14. The many-headed foam at Salamis.
15. Europe put off that foam when Phidias
16. Gave women dreams and dreams their looking-glass.

17. One image crossed the many-headed, sat
18. Under the tropic shade, grew round and slow,
19. No Hamlet thin from eating flies, a fat
20. Dreamer of the Middle Ages. Empty eyeballs knew
21. That knowledge increases unreality, that
22. Mirror on mirror mirrored is all the show.
23. When gong and conch declare the hour to bless
24. Grimalkin crawls to Buddha's emptiness.

25. When Pearse summoned Cuchulain to his side,
26. What stalked through the Post Office? What intellect,
27. What calculation, number, measurement, replied?
28. We Irish, born into that ancient sect
29. But thrown upon this filthy modern tide
30. And by its formless spawning fury wrecked,
31. Climb to our proper dark, that we may trace
32. The lineaments of a plummet-measured face.

ELLMANN says that 'Long-legged Fly' was composed in November 1937,[1] the year in which appeared the second, heavily revised, edition of *A Vision*. There remain two pages of manuscript working, which at the time of composition were in a loose-leaf notebook, and a single typescript. That these are not the earliest manuscript drafts is made clear by Edith Shackleton Heald's fascinating account of the genesis of this poem:

> Another of the poems he wrote here was 'The Long Legged Fly' which is published in the *Later Poems*, and he was thinking about that when I drove him over to see Lady Gerald Wellesley at Penns in the Rocks. It wasn't his first visit there—he was already great friends with Lady Gerald—when we were going round the garden with Lady Gerald, and Yeats noticed a kind of water-tortoise at the edge of a pool, and he asked Lady Gerald if it could swim. She said 'Oh yes, I suppose so.' He said 'Could I see it?' and she said 'Yes—let's throw it in.' And she asked me to throw it in and I did and it began to swim, but rather laboriously, it seemed, towards the shore. And Yeats said 'No—I don't think it'll do.' Afterwards, when we had come back home, he read the rough draft of a poem—this poem he'd been thinking about, called 'The Long-legged Fly'. It's about the necessity of silence and peace to people of creative energy: Caesar is one person and Michael Angelo is another, and he'd chosen the long-legged fly as the way it walks on the water being the way the creative mind moves upon silence. And when he'd read the poem to me, one line ran, 'Our master Caesar is in the tent where the maps are spread, His blue eyes fixed upon nothing.' Afterwards I said 'Would Caesar have blue eyes?' He said 'Oh, I don't know: how could I find out?' So I reached down Suetonius' *Life of the Caesars* and found some evidence that Caesar wouldn't have blue eyes, and now the line runs 'His eyes are fixed upon nothing'.[2]

On F. 1r Yeats wrote in ink, underlining each word of the refrain to indicate that it should be in italic:

---

[1] *The Identity of Yeats*, 1954, *p*. 294.

[2] *An interview with Bernard Price in 'Yeats in Sussex', broadcast by the B.B.C. on 4 September 1966.*

The Long Legged Fly

I

Quiet the dog, ~~Te~~ tether the poney

   To a distant post

Or civilization may perish

   Its great battle lost.

Ceasar is in his tent alone,

   Military maps are spread

His eye fixed upon nothing, ~~a hand~~
   A hand under his
   ~~Supporting the bloody~~ head

          <u>Like a long legged fly on the stream</u>

II

~~Show much politeness, gentleness~~

         <u>His mind moves upon silence</u>

~~Ceremony~~

II

Show much politeness, gentleness

   Ceremony in the place,
      the
Unless ~~those~~ topless are burned
     may
   Men ~~mus~~ lose that face.

She thinks, half woman half child,

   That nobody looks, her feet
     a
Dance to ~~some shuf~~ tinker's shuffle

  ~~Picked up in the street   Heard in some back street   Picked up~~
                       ~~in the street~~

<u>Like a long legged fly on the stream</u>

   <u>Her mind moves upon silence.</u>

III

Shut the door of the Pope's chapel

Keep those children out

Or girls at puberty may not find

The first Adam in their thought

There on the scaffolding reclines

Michael Angelo

With the sound that a mouse makes

His hand moves to and fro

Like a long legged fly on the stream

His mind moves upon silence

The workings on this page Yeats crossed out with a diagonal line before proceeding to F. 2r.

Long Legged Fly

I

That civilization may not ~~perish~~ sink

Its great battle lost

Quiet the dog, tether the pony

To a distant post,

~~Ceasar is in his tent alone~~ Our master Ceasar is in this tent
    ~~Where military~~
    ~~Military maps are spr spread~~ Where the maps are spread

His eyes fixed upon nothing

A hand under his head

Like a long legged fly upon ~~on the~~ the stream

His mind moves upon silence.

I

II

That
~~If~~ the topless towers may be ~~burn~~ burned,
    ~~That men~~ And men
    ~~Men~~ recal that face,

Show much politeness, gentleness

    Ceremony in this place;

She thinks half woman half child

    That nobody looks ~~(——.——)~~; her feet

Dancing to a tinker's shuffle
    She picked
    ~~Picked~~ up in the street

Like a long legged fly upon the stream

    Her mind moves upon silence

III

That girls at puberty may find

    The first Adam in their thought

Shut the door of the Pope's chapel

    ~~Keep~~ Keep those children out

There on that scaffolding reclines

    Michael Angelo

With no more sound than the mice make

    His hand moves to and fro

Like a long legged fly upon the stream

    His mind moves upon silence

Before examining in detail the changes between these drafts, it may be profitable to look at the poem's structure. This would seem to have been complete in Yeats's head, if not on paper (though this is likely), before these drafts were written. The poet, like a chorus figure, brings his reader within sight of a Roman general, Helen of Troy, and Michael Angelo: each of them is absorbed in a contemplative trance that must not be disturbed if his or her destiny is to be fulfilled. The reader or bystander is at once dramatically drawn into the poem: 'Quiet the dog . . .', 'Show much politeness . . .', 'Shut the door . . .'. He is given no time to notice that chronological sequence has been discarded—Roman Caesar coming before Grecian Helen—in favour of a poetically logical sequence. The impending and necessary battle of stanza I prepares for the necessary war and love of stanza II, which in turn prepares for the girls' necessary response to the artist's 'first Adam' in stanza III. This then is a poem about the heroic trinity of warrior, lover (in this case beloved), and artist; three facets of Yeats's ideal man. Of all his friends Major Robert Gregory seemed to him most nearly cast in that Renaissance mould:

> Our Sidney and our perfect man . . .
> Soldier, scholar, horseman, he,
> As 'twere all life's epitome.

To this ideal Yeats himself aspired, but, to his lasting regret, was never a man of action. We hear of him, however, brandishing Sato's Japanese sword and crying, 'Conflict, more conflict!'[1] A. E. Dyson has perceptively called attention to the fact that Caesar is here presented as the saviour of civilization, Helen as the destroyer of civilization, and Michael Angelo as the creator of civilization.[2]

> All things fall and are built again,
> And those that build them again are gay.

Subsidiary themes in 'Long-legged Fly' will emerge in an examination of Yeats's reshaping of his poem on F. 2r.

The major development here is the transposition in each stanza of the instruction to the onlooker ('Quiet the dog . . .', etc.) with the reason for that instruction ('That civilization may not sink . . .', etc.). As the desired end result is more important than the means

---

[1] Ellmann, op. cit., p. 8. See also 'A Dialogue of Self and Soul'.
[2] 'An Analysis of Yeats's "Long-legged Fly"', *The Critical Survey*, ii. 2 (1965), p. 102.

whereby it is achieved, properly it is put first, in the position of emphasis. In stanza I Caesar is in his tent, 'His eye fixed upon nothing'. This, as we might expect, is no gratuitous piece of information, but the application of one of the theories in *A Vision*:

> When I think of Rome I see always those heads with their world-considering eyes, and those bodies as conventional as the metaphors in a leading article, and compare in my imagination vague Grecian eyes gazing at nothing, Byzantine eyes of drilled ivory staring upon a vision, and those eyelids of China and of India, those veiled or half-veiled eyes weary of world and vision alike.[1]

It is curious that in 'Long-legged Fly' Yeats chose to make his visionary general a Roman Caesar, whose eyes we might expect to be 'world-considering', rather than a Greek, as it might be Alexander. Another instance of the visionary's empty eye occurs in 'The Statues':

> Empty eyeballs knew
> That knowledge increases unreality.

The refrain to this poem is at once one of Yeats's most audacious and successful. While on the literal plane a long-legged fly has little in common with Caesar, Helen, and Michael Angelo, it is an image that brilliantly fits their common state of mind. Drawn no doubt from the poet's experience as a fisherman, it is here peculiarly apt since the fly, distanced above the stream on its long legs, makes no more mark upon the water than the mind moving upon the silence.

There can be little question but that the tableau in stanza II of the child Helen dancing originates from an occasion when Yeats, holidaying in Normandy, discovered Iseult Gonne dancing upon the shore.

> My imagination goes some years backward, and I remember a beautiful young girl singing at the edge of the sea in Normandy words and music of her own composition. She thought herself alone, stood barefooted between sea and sand; sang with lifted head of the civilizations that there had come and gone, ending every verse with the cry: 'O Lord, let something remain'.[2]

---

[1] 1937 edition, p. 277.
[2] Ibid., pp. 219–20.

The sight would seem to have moved him deeply, since it prompted also 'To a Child Dancing in the Wind', 'Owen Aherne and his Dancers', and the central image of 'The Double Vision of Michael Robartes', that of the girl dancing between the figures of a Sphinx and a Buddha:

> For now being dead it seemed
> That she of dancing dreamed.
>
> Although I saw it all in the mind's eye
> There can be nothing solider till I die;
> I saw by the moon's light
> Now at its fifteenth night.

Here, as in 'Long-legged Fly', the girl turns out to be 'Homer's Paragon', but the point of greatest interest is that she dances by the light of the moon 'at its fifteenth night'. Space does not permit the rehearsal here of Yeats's theory of the twenty-eight phases of the moon, which is the core of *A Vision*. Suffice it to say that in this scheme the fifteenth phase, when all the moon is visible, diametrically opposes the first phase, when nothing is visible. The first phase represents total objectivity, the fifteenth total subjectivity. Human beings are said to belong to one or other of all the phases, with the exceptions of phases one and fifteen. Yeats calls the latter the 'phase of complete beauty', when 'Thought and Will are indistinguishable; and this is the consummation of a slow process; nothing is apparent but dreaming *Will* and the *Image* that it dreams'. Although the fifteenth phase of this 'Great Wheel' has no human embodiment, certain humans can yet attain to it in rare moments of remote exaltation: lovers, as in 'Solomon and the Witch'; the saint in beatific ecstasy; the artist, as Yeats himself in the poem 'Vacillation', 'when vision comes to our weariness like terrible lightning'. It is this state of lonely trance that Caesar, Helen, and Michael Angelo have in common in 'Long-legged Fly'. Here, as in 'The Double Vision of Michael Robartes', the girl is depicted dancing; the dance being Yeats's symbol for harmony, the complete marriage of thought and action.

The subject of stanza III Yeats had already touched on in

'Michael Robartes and the Dancer', and was to return to later in 'Under Ben Bulben':

> Michael Angelo left a proof
> On the Sistine Chapel roof,
> Where but half-awakened Adam
> Can disturb globe-trotting Madam
> Till her bowels are in heat.

The artist is not to be interrupted, lest he fail to complete the picture which in days to come will present its archetypal image of true and undistorted sexuality. In the closing lines of this stanza Yeats makes a telling alteration when he changes the phrase 'With the sound that a mouse makes', to 'With no more sound than the mice make.'

Yeats demanded, when engaged on a poem, the same conditions that he advocated for Michael Angelo. A letter written by Sir Ian Hamilton in 1908 gave a lively picture of the poet at work at Coole Park:

> Yeats and I were the only guests in the big house. Yeats unfortunately for my enjoyment was in the throes of composition and was being thoroughly spoilt. No one can ever have heard anyone play up to him like Lady Gregory. His bedroom was halfway down a passage on the first floor at the end of which was my room. All along the passage for some distance on either side of Yeats's door were laid thick rugs to prevent the slightest sound reaching the holy of holies—Yeats's bed.[1]

'Long-legged Fly' reaches its final form, except for one word, punctuation, and a roman refrain detached from each stanza, in its one typescript. Every change is towards greater compression: in line 5, 'this tent' becomes 'the tent'; in line 11, 'may be burned' becomes 'be burnt'; and lines 13 and 14,

> *Show much politeness, gentleness*
> *Ceremony in this place;*

are completely recast as:

> Move most gently if move you must
> In this lonely place.

[1] J. M. Hone, *W. B. Yeats, 1865–1939*, 1942, p. 225.

The latter version is much more realistically in keeping with the dramatic situation: politeness, gentleness and ceremony[1] are more Renaissance than Homeric qualities.[2] In line 15, 'half woman half child' becomes the more rhythmical 'part woman, three parts a child'; leaving only line 18, 'Picked up on the street', to be changed in the finished poem to 'Picked up on a street'.

The muscular, ballad rhythms of the finished poem conceal, like simple flesh, a structural organism of considerable complexity.

2

In Yeats's *Last Poems* 'The Statues' is dated 9 April 1938; Ellmann dates it 22 June of that year; a version was sent with a covering letter to Edith Shackleton Heald on 28 June;[3] and Yeats himself wrote at the head of the poem's last typescript, 'Final Version Sept 23'. These discrepancies, which simply represent different stages in the poem's development, are important only in that they indicate that this development took six months. It is possible to plot the growth of 'The Statues' more fully than that of 'Long-legged Fly'. Though several early pages would seem to have been lost, there remain six sheets of preliminary manuscript working, which at the time of composition were in a loose-leaf notebook; a full draft of the poem on two further sheets; and six typescripts. This said, there must be added a proviso that the sequence of F. 1r to F. 6v is difficult to reconstruct with certainty, and in these Yeats's handwriting is more than usually hard to read. I have a strong suspicion that in these early workings he did not begin with stanza I and proceed to stanzas II, III, and IV in that order: but in the

---

[1] The word 'ceremony' had important associations for Yeats: compare 'The ceremony of innocence is drowned'; ('The Second Coming'), and ('A Prayer for my Daughter'):

How but in custom and in ceremony
Are innocence and beauty born?

[2] B. C. Southam's ingenious theory, that the speaker in the second stanza is a Greek soldier watching Helen from within the wooden horse, is not supported by the earlier form of these lines. See his 'Yeats: Life and the Creator in "Long-legged Fly"', *Twentieth Century Literature*, vi (1961), pp. 175-9. See also James L. Allen's comment on Southam's article, 'Yeats's "Long-legged Fly"', *Explicator*, xxi (1963), item 51; and Southam's reply, 'Yeats's "Long-legged Fly"', *Explicator*, xxii (1964).

[3] A. Wade, ed., *The Letters of W. B. Yeats*, 1954, p. 911.

1. F. 1r of 'The Statues': see page 125 for transcription.

absence of conclusive proof, and because it will make the pattern of the poem easier to follow, I am assuming that he did. F. 1r is a preliminary prose draft:

I

They went out in broad day or under the moon

Moving with ~~the~~ dream certainty, somebody calls them

(. .); ~~only forms incapable of~~ empty faces,

measured Pythagorean perfection; only that which is

incapable of thought is infinite in passion; only passion

sees God. Men were victorious at Salamis, & human

victories are nothing, now one up, then another; &

only those cold marble forms could drive
      the
back the vague, asiatic hoard; ~~we have all~~ things
          multiform
~~Victory Europe. Only their certainty could~~ beat down Nature

with their certainty

II

Weary of victory ~~that which men had give it~~

one was far from all his companions—& sat so long
      once athletic
in solitude, that his body became soft & round
           incapable of work
but ~~before his empty eye God in his empty eye~~ or war,

because his eyes were empty, ~~that the most~~ more empty

than the skies at night more empty than the sky

than any thing man can image all men worshipped forms

deity. ~~Appolo had taken the name of~~ Buddha
    Apolo
~~Oppolo~~ forgot Pythagoras & took the name of Buddha

> *which was victorious Greece in the Asiatic (.   ). Others*
>
> *had stayed away & were (.   .   .   .) asiatic (.   )*
>
> *their sublime emptiness, & in a purple night (.   ) they saw*
>
> *marble put forth many heads & feet*

Beneath this Yeats wrote *P.T.O.* and continued on F. 1*v*:

III

> *Where are you now. Is it true that you shed the*
>
> *sun–burn & became pale white; Did you appear*
>
> *in the Post Office in 1916 is it True that*
>
> *Pearse called on you by name of Cuchullain*
>
> *Certainty we have need of you. The vague flood is at its*
>
> *Height from one quarter ~~alo~~ alone, from all four quarters is coming*
>
> *Come back with all your Pythagorean numbers*

Already uppermost in the poet's mind is the conflict between the systematized 'certainty' of the Greeks (as represented by their sculpture based on the mathematical principles of Pythagoras) and 'the vague, asiatic hoard' [horde]. On a more general level, 'Europe and Asia were [for Yeats] new representations of the subjective and objective gyres'.[1] The reference to 'multiform Nature' in this prose draft underlines Vivienne Koch's statement that 'Yeats saw Asia as a vast female principle or "Nature"'.[2] In 'The Statues' he attributes the Greeks' overthrowal of the Persians more to the character of Greek thought and art than to their force of arms as displayed at the naval battle of Salamis in 480 B.C. Edward Engelberg, in a learned and illuminating discussion of this poem,[3] shows Yeats indebted for his theme to Pater, who found the 'full

---

[1] Ellmann, *The Identity of Yeats*, 1954, p. 190.

[2] *W. B. Yeats, The Tragic Phase*, 1951. Her chapter on this poem provides a full and helpful exegesis.

[3] *The Vast Design*, 1964, p. 189.

2. F. 1v of 'The Statues': see page 126 for transcription.

expression of . . . humanism', man with a sense of 'inward value', embodied in the marbles of Aegina:

> In this monument, then, we have a revelation in the sphere of art, of the temper which made the victories of Marathon and Salamis possible, of the true spirit of Greek chivalry as displayed in the Persian war, and in the highly ideal conceptions of its events . . .[1]

This 'temper' was later to be superimposed by Alexander and his followers on the thought and culture of Persia and northern India. The Ghandara Buddhas of the North-West Frontier have profiles and drapery as conspicuously Greek as many statues in the museums of Athens. Yeats sees Cuchulain as a spiritual descendant, or reincarnation of Apollo and Buddha. These themes he explores further, on F. 2r, in a prose passage that was to appear, in its finished form, in *On the Boiler* (p. 37):

~~because of the overthrow of the Persian galleys~~

Europe was not born, when Greek galleys defeated the

the Persian hords at Salamis, but when the doric

studios sent out those broad backed marble statues

[2]   *and empty, empty because altogether*

[2] *Those faces which are drawn ~~because all thought is emptied & measured~~*

[2]   *(. . . . .),*   *~~even those empty faces~~*

[2]   *~~numbers~~*

[2]   *mathematics*

Which carry out in plastic art the ~~genius~~ of Pythagoras
              expressive

against the multiform vague asiatic sea. They gave to the

sexual instinct of Europe its goal, its fixed type. ~~Along~~

~~the French & Italian riviera~~ In the warm sea of the
            Riviera

French & Italian ~~riviera we~~ one can still see it

I recall a Swedish actress standing upon some

boat's edge between Porto Fino & Rapallo, & riding the

foam upon a plank toed behind a speed (.) or speed boat

---

[1] *Greek Studies*, 1895, pp. 269, 273.
[2] Indicates a line inserted from the top of the page.

but ~~it everywhere~~ one finds ~~& everywhere~~ & where ever

the lucky or the wealthy uncover their sunburnt bodies, there
 all
are the doric proportions, & ~~those~~ doubtless those

flesh tints that greek painters loved, as have all the

greatest since ; no where upon any beautiful body, whether
       patches whereby
a man or woman, those red ~~patches~~ our democratic

painters prove that they have really studied from

life

The final version of this passage in *On the Boiler* is preceded by a
sentence that is relevant to stanza IV of 'The Statues': 'There are
moments when I am certain that art must once again accept those
Greek proportions which carry into plastic art the Pythagorean
numbers, those faces which are divine because all there is empty
and measured.' In his essay 'Ireland After The Revolution' in the
same magazine, Yeats goes further: 'let every schoolmaster . . .
teach Irish and Greek together, make the pupil translate Greek into
Irish, Irish into Greek . . . Mathematics should be taught, because
being certainty without reality it is the modern key to power . . .'.
  On F. 2*v* the verse drafts of stanza I begin with a marked repetition of the word 'moon', which suggests that the 'system' of *A
Vision* lies near the surface of the poet's mind:

In doric marble cold as moon or star

   or chill of moon & star ~~a star~~

 ~~Under broad day or under the moon the moon, came~~

 ~~Every thing measured every thing understood~~
        ~~(.)~~ place moving
 ~~Pythagorean marble numbers on slate, on slate~~
  ~~natural~~
 ~~The human & the certain mingled there,~~
  ~~all~~   *in imagined*
But *Boys & girls the ~~uncommited~~ love*

Of lonely beds knew what

Of solitary beds knew what they are

can
Nor ask for character in limb or face And that perfection may be warm
enough

The place of passion is an empty (.) place

Nor say that measurement is not enough
  Though they lack character
Nor lack for character in limb & face

The place of passion is an empty place

Like moon & star the doric marbles move

Below this Yeats rearranges the stanza's opening lines, and begins
again:

The natural & the certain mingled there
                doric
Those difficult Pythagorean numbers move
  In marble or bronze to get mankind to stare Make the people stare
In doric marble cold as moon or star

But boys and girls in the imagined love

Of solitary beds knew what they are
  That plummet measured forms have life enough
And that perfection can be warm enough That measured heads can have
    they
Though it lack character in face & limb & face
                    (. .)
The place of passion is an empty place
              (.) That passion is an empty
        (. . . .) empty place
[1] *That passion could burn all but empty space*

On F. *3r* he continues to work at stanza I:

            permanent & the imagined
        The natural & the certain mingle there

        Pythagorean numbers seemed to live & move

---

[1] Indicates a line inserted, at the barb of a swooping arrow, from the centre of the page.

On marble or ~~in~~ bronze the ⟨——.——⟩ stupid people stare

But boys & girls in the imagined love

Of solitary beds knew what they are

That ~~Plum~~ plummet measured forms are (.) ~~en~~ enough

Though it lack character in ~~face &~~ limb & face
     can burn
That passion could ~~consume~~ an empty place

[1] *That passion can be character enough*

[1] *All other kinds corrupt a limb or face*

[1] *That (.) the gods desert a crowded place*

  No
~~A~~ greater than Pythagoras! The man
     who made these measurements upon a slate,
Who in some doric studio discovered these,

These calculations that are flesh, put down
    sensitive
All Asiatic ~~vague~~ immensities

And not those banks of oars that rode upon

The many headed foam at Salamis
 ~~⟨——.——⟩~~
~~⟨——.——.——⟩ Phidias, but Phidias~~
  ~~dreams &~~
~~Gave dreams gave women their looking glass~~
   &
Gave women ~~dreams~~ dreams ~~& dreams~~ their looking glass
 And victory out ran (.)
His victory runs on ⟨——.——⟩ for Phidias

Gave women dreams & dreams their looking glass

A greater than Pythagoras for the men
    all this
Who made these numbers upon a slate ~~though those~~ those
  look but
Calculations that ~~seem but~~ casual flesh put down

  [1] Indicates a line inserted from the top of the page.

Here stanza II makes its first, and already well-developed, appearance in stanza form. The poet's rhetorically effective but none the less cryptic denial, 'No [!] greater than Pythagoras!', Vivienne Koch paraphrases as:

I said in stanza one that Pythagoras was responsible for the principles incarnated in the perfection of Greek statues. But I have now changed my mind. It was not Pythagoras who did this, but rather the actual artists . . .

The idea of Phidias's statues giving women dreams presents an interesting parallel with the effects of Michael Angelo's painted ceiling in 'Long-legged Fly'.

    F. 3*v* contains a few scribbled jottings for stanza III:

> *Knew*
> ~~*Our (.)*~~
> ~~*Our Hamlet was*~~
> *Our Hamlet thinks, (. .) hand can ble*
>
> *Budda has found a great emptiness*
>
> *From eating flies, but a fat medeval fool*
>
> *No Hamlet thin from eating flies a fat*
>
> *Medeval fool*
>   *Hamlet thin*

On F. 4*r* Yeats returns to the troublesome stanza I:

>   *I*
>
>   *studios*
> *The doric statues made the people stare*
>
> ~~*The*~~ *Pythagorean numbers had begun to move*
>   *For*   *had mingled*
> ~~*The*~~ *nature & certainty* ~~*had*~~ *comingled there*
>   *and the imagined love*
> *In bronze or in Marble* ~~*but*~~ *the imagined love*
>   *knew what they*
> *Of solitary beds knew what they were*
>
> *That passion could be character enough*

> *And pressed under dark night's empty space*
>
> ~~*Lips upon*~~ *Live lips upon a plummet measured face*
>
> *The Doric studios had made the people stare*
>
> ~~*Pythagorean numbers seemed upon the move*~~
>
> ~~*Pythagorean numerals*~~
>
> *How (.) give Pythagorean numbers on the move*
>   *in*   ~~*that*~~
> *In Marble or Bronze a human air,*
>
> ~~*But boys & girls in the imagined love*~~
>
> ~~*Of solitary beds knew what they were*~~
>
> *Could there be human. The imagined love*
>
> *Of solitary beds knew what they were*
>
> *That passion could give character enough*
>
> *And pressed*

With this draft, the second half of stanza I advances a stage nearer
its final form.

On F. 5*r* he explores the substance of what was to be stanza III:

> ~~*A form went east*~~
>   ~~*moved east ward*~~
> ~~*One form went east*~~
>   *(. .) many headed*
>   *Under (. . .) & sat*
> *One form,* ~~*went through the eastern (.) east*~~
>
> ~~*Among the mango groves*~~
>   ~~*his body*~~
> *Under a mango,* ~~*& grew fat soft &*~~ *round & slow*
>
> *No Hamlet thin from eating flies* ~~*a fat*~~ *a fat*
>
> *Medeval fool; his measured eye balls know*
>
> *All* ~~*(. . . . .)*~~
>
> *(.)* ~~*full & empty all the same & thinks that*~~ *(.)*

~~*What all the measurements are*~~ (.) *&*

               knowledge is not reality (.)

~~*What drives the sun & moon & thinks*~~

All the illustrious gods are but a show

   ~~(.) *something & nothing are*~~

~~*That there is nothing to be known & tho*~~

All the illustrious gods are but a show

Knowledge is not reality & though

All the illustrious gods are but a show

And thinks his hand alone knew how to bless

A Hamlet knows of that great emptiness

As several critics have observed, a memory of Morris informs the present stanza. Here, from *Autobiographies*, is the description of his portrait painted by Watts, and it is clear that the detail of the prose constituted an image-cluster of great importance to Yeats himself:[1]

A reproduction of his portrait by Watts hangs over my mantelpiece with Henley's, and those of other friends. Its grave wide-open eyes, like the eyes of some dreaming beast, remind me of the open eyes of Titian's *Ariosto*, while the broad vigorous body suggests a mind that has no need of the intellect to remain sane, though it give itself to every fantasy: the dreamer of the Middle Ages. It is 'the fool of Faery . . . wide and wild as a hill', the resolute European image that yet half remembers Buddha's motionless meditation, and has no trait in common with the wavering, lean image of hungry speculation, that cannot but because of certain famous Hamlets of our stage fill the mind's eye. Shakespeare himself foreshadowed a symbolic change, that is, a change in the whole temperament of the world, for though he called his Hamlet 'fat' and even 'scant of breath', he thrust between his fingers agile rapier and dagger.[2]

F. 5*v* contains a draft of part of 'The Man and the Echo'. Stanza IV would seem to have been sketched for the first time in verse form on F. 6*v*:[3]

    What measure ment ~~*went out a human limb face*~~

    ~~*And called it self* (. .) *name & stood*~~

---

[1] F. A. C. Wilson, *Yeats's Iconography*, 1960, p. 300.

[2] *Autobiographies*, 1955, pp. 141–2.   [3] F. 6*r* contains a draft of the poem 'Politics'.

~~By Pearse in the post office~~

What Pythagorean measure ment appeared
(.)
~~Came~~ *to the Post office & stood at Pearse's side*
~~That grew very~~
And called it self Cuchuchlain. ~~Gods have I heard,~~ someone they heard

~~The (. .)~~

~~H A half crazy cry I call~~
That
~~This~~ *half crazy (.) up I call, ~~& far & wide~~ Have we not heard*

~~(.) all the people (. . .)~~

~~By the~~

~~From (.),~~

(.) the many limbs & heads (. .)

~~And can compare limbs legs (.)~~

~~That compare limbs legs~~

And compare limbs & although the birds

~~And that amid such dark & empty space~~

That we ~~in those amid~~ under this dark high empty

May find a head and plummet measured face

As there remain no further loose-leaf sheets of rough manuscript working, we must assume that Yeats moved on to his first complete draft on F. 7r:

Pythagorean Numbers

were   *should the*
What ~~are~~ those images? ~~there~~ Why ~~did~~ people stare
~~The Doric studios made the people stare~~
Did ~~doric studios~~
~~Why did those images make the people stare?~~
                    seemed
Pythagorean numbers though they seemed to move

3. F. 7r of 'The Statues': see pages 135, 137, and 139 for transcription.

                                    lacked
 In   *In marble or in bronze ~~lack~~ character*
        Did ~~But~~ boys & girls in the
        ~~Therefore humanity.~~ The imagined love
                                    knew
        Of solitary beds ~~know~~ what they ~~are~~ were ;
 Know   *~~Knew~~ could*
        ~~That~~ passion ~~can~~ be character enough ;
                Press
        ~~Pressed~~ under the dark night's empty ~~sp~~ place

        Live lips upon a plummet measured face.

                         II

        No
        ~~And~~ not Pythagoras but a greater, for the ~~man~~ men
                those numbers
        Who made ~~these measurements~~ on a slate, or moulded these
        Calculations that look but casual flesh
        ~~Images~~ ~~that are numbers & flesh~~ put down

        All Asiatic vague iménsities

        And not those oar banked gallies that rode upon

        The many headed sea at Salamis ;
                    its drops
            Europe put off ~~this foam~~ when
        Nor ~~lack their spirit & measurement~~, Phideas

        Gave women dreams & dreams their looking glass

                         III

                ~~Water sea a~~
        One image crossed the ~~narrow sea & sat~~ many headed, sat
        ~~Amid the tropic shade but it~~ under the temple shade,
        ~~So long in the sun that it~~ grew round & slow,

        Not Hamlet thin from eating flies, ~~but~~ a fat   ~~ages ;~~
                ~~(.);~~   dreamer of the middle ages ;
        ~~Medieval fool. Its measured eye balls knew~~   knew
                        his dropped eyes & ~~know~~
        That knowledge increases unreality, that

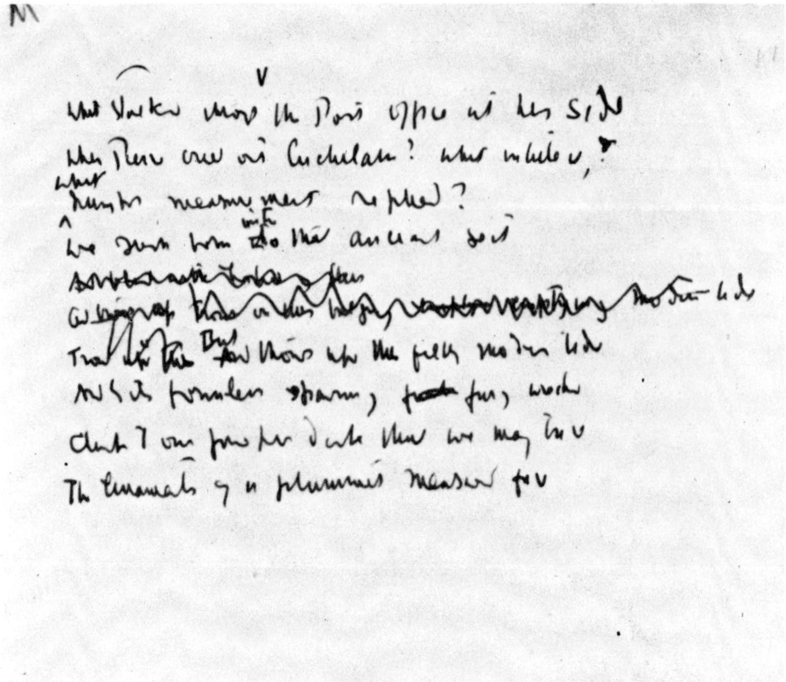

4. F. 8*r* of 'The Statues': see page 139 for transcription.

Mirror on mirror mirrored is all the show.

~~*And that its hand alone knows how to b*~~   *When gong & conch resound*
                                        that he may bless
That ~~only Buddha's hand knew how to bless~~   *hand*
                                ~~*That Budd hand*~~ *indifferent* ~~*hand*~~
~~*And Hamlet knew to the great emptiness*~~   *knew how to bless*

Grimalkin kneels to Buddha's emptiness

F. 8r: *V*

 What stalked through the Post office at his side

 When Pearse cried out Cuchulain? What intellect,
  What
 Numbers measurement replied?
    into
 We Irish born ~~to~~ that ancient sect

 ~~*And (.   .   .   .   .   .   )*~~

 ~~*And thrown up thrown on this vulgar empty emptying modern tide*~~
   But
 ~~*Thrown upon this And*~~ *thrown upon this filthy modern tide*

 And by its formless spawning ~~fury~~ fury wrecked

 Climb to our proper dark that we may trace

 The lineaments of a plummet measured face

Several lines of stanzas I and II are here improved or attain their final form:

Line 1. What were those images? Why should the people stare
 7.   . . . the dark night's empty place
 11. Calculations that look but casual flesh . . .
 13. And not those oar banked gallies that rode upon

Stanza III of this complete draft is so great an advance on F. 5r, and stanza IV so great an advance on F. 6v, that there can be little doubt that some intermediate pages of manuscript are missing. The 'image' that now makes its first appearance in stanza II refers back to the images sculptured by Phidias in line 1. This crosses 'the narrow sea' (presumably the Bosphorus or the Dardanelles), a phrase that Yeats cancels in favour of 'the many headed', which is of course an echo of line 14. 'The mango groves' of F. 5r have now given place to 'the temple shade'; and gong, conch, and Grimalkin enter the poem for the first time. I know of no more satisfactory interpretation of the obscure symbol of the witch's cat than that of F. A. C. Wilson, who paraphrases lines 23 and 24 as follows:

> The modern Indian worshipper, who has been caught up in the materialist 'tide' and has become almost wholly objective, so that his true gods are the witch's cat and the dragon-monster of Eastern art, even today at the hour of prayer is ironically compelled to pay homage to subjective religion.[1]

This reading is supported by Yeats's attack on modern egalitarian India in *On the Boiler*: 'the new-formed democratic parliaments of India will doubtless destroy, if they can, the caste system that has saved Indian intellect.'

Stanza V on F. 8r is written with the boldness and rapidity that often in Yeats's manuscripts suggest the urgency of inspiration. It may well be that the poem's superb, prophetic climax and close sprang fully-formed on to the paper. He begins from the idea expressed also in 'Under Ben Bulben':

> Measurement began our might:
> Forms a stark Egyptian thought,
> Forms that gentler Phidias wrought.

Though heirs to this heritage, the Irish are now wrecked upon a 'modern tide' as 'formless' as the 'many headed', 'multiform vague asiatic sea'. By discovering like Yeats himself, or rediscovering, a system of formal order, they will initiate a new cycle of civilization; climbing to the darkness in which one historical gyre dies and another is born. 'After an age of necessity, truth, goodness, mechanism, science, democracy, abstraction, peace', he wrote in *A Vision*, 'comes an age of freedom, fiction, evil, kindred, art, particularity, war. Our age has burned to the socket.' The logic of the poem

---

[1] *Yeats's Iconography*, 1960, p. 301.

implies a parallel between the battles of Salamis and the Dublin
Post Office. By 1938, of course, the insurgents' defeat was seen as a
moral victory, and there can be little doubt that Yeats is further
implying that in this the Irish artists played a part comparable to
that he attributes to the Greek artists in preparing for the victory
at Salamis. Nor is this proud claim without some justification, for
the Irish literary revival did undoubtedly help to shape the
nationalism that reached its climax at Easter 1916.

'The Statues' received its final polishing in four ink-corrected
typescripts. On F. 9r twelve lines are tightened:

Line 4.   . . . pale from the imagined love
      7. And press at midnight in some public place
      9. A greater than Pythagoras for the men
     14. The many-headed foam . . .
     15. Europe put off this foam . . .
     19. No Hamlet . . .
     20. Dreamer of the middle-ages. Empty eyeballs knew
     23. When gong and conch declare the hour to bless
     24. Grimalkin crawls to Buddha's emptiness.
     25. When Pearse summoned Cuchullain to his side
     26. What stalked through the post office? What intellect,
     27. What calculation, number, measurement, replied?

By inserting 'calculation' into line 27, and presumably resisting the
temptation to delete 'number', Yeats made it an alexandrine—the
only one in the poem. On F. 10r the title 'Pythagorean Numbers'
is changed to 'The Statues', which is clearly more suitable, and the
first two lines of stanzas I and II respectively are altered:

      1. Pythagoras made these. Why did the people stare?
      2. His numbers though they moved, or seemed to move
      9. No greater than Pythagoras! The men
     10. Who totted on a slate, or modelled these

Four lines achieve their final form on F. 11r:

      1. Pythagoras planned it. Why did the people stare?
      6. That passion could bring . . .
      7. And pressed . . .
     10. That with a mallet or a chisel modelled these

and one on F. 12r:

> 9. No greater than Pythagoras for the men

Another line there received its last but one correction:

> 13. And not those banks of oars that swam upon

Save for the substitution of 'the' for 'those' in line 13 and changes of punctuation, that were more probably made by the poet's wife or publisher, 'The Statues' was now complete.

Vivienne Koch describes in her Foreword the principles of her critical method of approach:

> first, a willingness to let that particular poem take hold of the imagination as if it were—at the moment of scrutiny—the only poem in the world; second, to let only that particular poem and no other source—whether in poetry or prose—determine, *in so far as it is possible*,[1] what its meaning is.

This is, of course, a method developed by modern critics and applied often with success. As with surgery, however, where the operation that cures one patient can kill another, the critical method that illuminates one poem will fail to illuminate another. Miss Koch, significantly, is at her best where she departs most radically from the critical principles she advocates; and for one all-important reason. It was a dominant concern of Yeats as a writer 'to hammer his thoughts into unity'. To adopt, therefore, a critical approach that ignores the organic nature of his work and the fact that many poems may be members of one body, in that they share one symbolic skeleton, is to deny that the poet either meant what he said or achieved what he intended. As he wrote in his Preface to the 1899 edition of his poems: 'I must leave my myths and images to explain themselves as the years go by and one poem lights up another.' This, says Miss Koch in effect, we must not allow them to do. Rather, we must isolate each in a soundproof operating theatre and, ignoring all previous case-histories, fall to with our scalpel.

While she is right that the critic must concentrate on the poem before him, this act of purging the consciousness of its awareness of other poems, of other forms of experience, is as perverse to attempt as it is impossible to fulfil. A mind that has mastered *A*

---

[1] The italics in this important escape clause are Miss Koch's own.

Vision, let us say, cannot or should not empty itself of this understanding, any more than the eye reading a particular line can or should obliterate the impression of lines above and below it.

An intelligent reader, but one who had never read poem or prose by Yeats before, might 'make sense' of 'Long-legged Fly' or 'The Statues' if confronted with it for the first time; but much less sense than the reader who had. Miss Koch herself says, 'to obstruct the use of electric light merely because one wants to prove that one *can* read by candle-light is a wasteful pastime'. Study of the development of these poems demonstrates that one poem does light up another, and though, of course, not all the prose lights up all the poems, much of it lights up many. Therefore, if we want to understand part of the *opus* we must read the whole—chronologically, if possible. We should perhaps allow the last word to Yeats himself, who dedicated his *Autobiographies* to 'Those few people mainly personal friends who have read all that I have written'.

VI

UNDER BEN BULBEN

••

I

1. Swear by what the sages spoke
2. Round the Mareotic Lake
3. That the Witch of Atlas knew,
4. Spoke and set the cocks a-crow.

5. Swear by those horsemen, by those women
6. Complexion and form prove superhuman,
7. That pale, long-visaged company
8. That air in immortality
9. Completeness of their passions won;
10. Now they ride the wintry dawn
11. Where Ben Bulben sets the scene.

12. Here's the gist of what they mean.

II

13. Many times man lives and dies
14. Between his two eternities,
15. That of race and that of soul,
16. And ancient Ireland knew it all.
17. Whether man die in his bed
18. Or the rifle knocks him dead,
19. A brief parting from those dear
20. Is the worst man has to fear.

21. Though grave-diggers' toil is long,
22. Sharp their spades, their muscles strong,
23. They but thrust their buried men
24. Back in the human mind again. -

III

25. You that Mitchel's prayer have heard,
26. 'Send war in our time, O Lord!'
27. Know that when all words are said
28. And a man is fighting mad,
29. Something drops from eyes long blind,
30. He completes his partial mind,
31. For an instant stands at ease,
32. Laughs aloud, his heart at peace.
33. Even the wisest man grows tense
34. With some sort of violence
35. Before he can accomplish fate,
36. Know his work or choose his mate.

IV

37. Poet and sculptor, do the work,
38. Nor let the modish painter shirk
39. What his great forefathers did,
40. Bring the soul of man to God,
41. Make him fill the cradles right.

42. Measurement began our might:
43. Forms a stark Egyptian thought,
44. Forms that gentler Phidias wrought.
45. Michael Angelo left a proof
46. On the Sistine Chapel roof,
47. Where but half-awakened Adam
48. Can disturb globe-trotting Madam

49. Till her bowels are in heat,
50. Proof that there's a purpose set
51. Before the secret working mind:
52. Profane perfection of mankind.

53. Quattrocento put in paint
54. On backgrounds for a God or Saint
55. Gardens where a soul's at ease;
56. Where everything that meets the eye,
57. Flowers and grass and cloudless sky,
58. Resemble forms that are or seem
59. When sleepers wake and yet still dream,
60. And when it's vanished still declare,
61. With only bed and bedstead there,
62. That heavens had opened.
                               Gyres run on;
63. When that greater dream had gone
64. Calvert and Wilson, Blake and Claude,
65. Prepared a rest for the people of God,
66. Palmer's phrase, but after that
67. Confusion fell upon our thought.

V

68. Irish poets, learn your trade,
69. Sing whatever is well made,
70. Scorn the sort now growing up
71. All out of shape from toe to top,
72. Their unremembering hearts and heads
73. Base-born products of base beds.
74. Sing the peasantry, and then
75. Hard-riding country gentlemen,
76. The holiness of monks, and after
77. Porter-drinkers' randy laughter;
78. Sing the lords and ladies gay
79. That were beaten into the clay

80. Through seven heroic centuries;
81. Cast your mind on other days
82. That we in coming days may be
83. Still the indomitable Irishry.

VI

84. Under bare Ben Bulben's head
85. In Drumcliff churchyard Yeats is laid.
86. An ancestor was rector there
87. Long years ago, a church stands near,
88. By the road an ancient cross.
89. No marble, no conventional phrase;
90. On limestone quarried near the spot
91. By his command these words are cut:

92. *Cast a cold eye*
93. *On life, on death.*
94. *Horseman, pass by!*

IN 1938 Yeats was seventy-three and increasingly aware that he had months rather than years to live.

> 'The work is done,' grown old he thought,
> 'According to my boyish plan;
> Let the fools rage, I swerved in nought,
> Something to perfection brought . . .'

'Something to perfection brought'—the elegy for example. 'In Memory of Major Robert Gregory', 'Upon a Dying Lady', 'Easter 1916', 'In Memory of Eva Gore-Booth and Con Markiewicz', and 'Coole Park 1929' had established him as one of the greatest elegists in the English language. At seventy-three he had only one elegy left to write: his own.

Hone says that a prose draft of 'Under Ben Bulben' was written in August 1938 and the final version read to F. R. Higgins on the night before Yeats left Ireland for the last time. Higgins, in fact, would not have heard the *final* version, as Hone tells us that on Thursday, 26 January 1939 Yeats 'rallied towards nightfall and gave Mrs. Yeats corrections for "Under Ben Bulben"'. On Saturday, 28 January he died at two in the afternoon.[1]

It is possible to date the conception of the poem yet more closely, since on 15 August 1938 Yeats wrote to Dorothy Wellesley from Riversdale:

. . . I have found a book of essays about Rilke waiting me; one on Rilke's ideas about death annoyed me. I wrote on the margin:

> Draw rein; draw breath.
> Cast a cold eye
> On life, on death.
> Horseman pass by.[2]

Mrs. Yeats's recollection of this incident is somewhat different. One morning when, as was his habit, he was working in bed, she heard him call, and entered his room to see him hurl to the floor in disgust

---

[1] Joseph Hone, *W. B. Yeats, 1865-1939*, p. 477.
[2] A. Wade, ed., *The Letters of W. B. Yeats*, p. 913.

the book of essays on Rilke. He did not then write in the book's
margin, she tells me, the quatrain that was to become his epitaph,
but on a scrap of paper. This first draft I believe to have been lost,
though there does remain a quarto sheet of typing-paper on which
is written, in ink:

Horse man

Draw rein; draw breath.

Cast a cold eye

On life, on death.

Horse man pass by.

The title suggests that, at this stage at least, it was considered as a
separate poem. Another version of these lines on F. 7r of the 'Under
Ben Bulben' drafts,[1] in which 'Turn that indifferent eye' is corrected to 'Cast a cold eye', would seem to indicate that by 15 August
when he wrote to Dorothy Wellesley Yeats had already begun
'Under Ben Bulben'. The last line of his quatrain suggests the
influence—whether conscious or unconscious it is impossible to
say—of the words '*Abi viator*' in Swift's epitaph. We know that
Yeats considered this 'the greatest . . . in history'.

There remain twenty-six folios of manuscript and typescript
working, not counting the draft of the epitaph cited above: these
show that the composition of 'Under Ben Bulben' fell into four
phases. First, on nine folios of a small loose-leaf notebook Yeats
made three very rough prose drafts. Then on two more folios in the
same notebook his poem starts to stumble into rhyme. Phase three
is a complete, but rough, verse draft on six folios of a large loose-leaf
notebook. Finally there are three typescripts, each of three quarto
sheets. The prose drafts are very rough indeed: many words are—
to me, at any rate—illegible. The problem of transcription is further
complicated by the fact that Yeats at this stage was thinking on
paper. His sentences are often unfinished, left in the air, as his mind
changes direction.

[1] See below, p. 158.

L

F. 1r is entitled 'Creed' and begins, not surprisingly, 'I believe':

Creed

I

I believe what the old saints

a thousand years before Christ, sitting under

the palms, like the old saints about

the Mareotic sea. ~~that~~ *From eternity*

through eternity to eternity man moves.

I believe with the men upon the road

& the common men that there are

(. .) play (. . . .)

the newly dead show themselves

here & there, or sport there above

(. .)

[1] *I have desired what the proffets*

[1] *know or sages that (.)*

[1] *among old women & beggar men*

II

I believe that there is nothing to fear

that ~~death & pain are dreadful~~

~~Yet I shake to hear the word when~~

The 'old saints a thousand years before Christ, sitting under the palms' I take to be a reference to the priests of, first, Apollo and,

---

[1] Indicates a line inserted, at the pointing of an arrow, from the top of the page.

secondly, Buddha. In the drafts of 'The Statues', a poem whose
composition partially overlapped with 'Under Ben Bulben', occurs
the sentence 'Appolo had taken the name of Buddha'.[1] In Yeats's
cyclic view of history one religion rises as another falls. Apollo and
Dionysus prefigure Buddha, who prefigures Christ, who prefigures
the 'rough beast' of 'The Second Coming', 'slouching towards
Bethlehem to be born'. So here, the priests of pre-Christian eras are
followed by 'the old saints about the Mareotic sea'. It is almost
certain that Yeats first read of S. Anthony and Egyptian monasticism
of the third and fourth centuries in two books by J. O. Hannay:
The Spirit and Origin of Christian Monasticism (1903) and *The
Wisdom of the Desert* (1904). From the beliefs of the early Christian
monks, Yeats turns in this first prose draft to the beliefs of 'the men
upon the road . . . old women and beggar men'. The road, of course,
is an Irish road, and he is affirming his faith in the pagan mythology
of Ireland. So from the drafts of 'The Statues' it is clear that Yeats
regarded Cuchulain as the spiritual descendant of Apollo. Where the
Christian begins his Creed 'I believe in one God,' Yeats is sympa-
thetic to any religion that believes in a life of the soul after death.

F. *2r* continues the first prose draft:

> *where (.   .   .   .   .) becomes (.   .   .)*
>
> *armed philosophers seek each other in*
>
> *air, where the conflict is has be*
>
> *becomes nobility of body*
>
> *Neither for those who die in bed who die at*
>
> *battle field. I believe that if there was*
>
> *anything to fear that great will of the*
>
> *world could not exist with the eternal laughter*
>
> *eternal joy. To that joy & that laughter*
>
> *I gave my life—I am old & ill*

[1] See p. 125.

> *my flesh is heavy it weighs upon my*
>
> *heart but I shall soon cast it off*
>
> *be ~~as light as~~ if god wills I shall*
>
> *be as light as a bird (. .).*

Yeats cancelled this page with diagonal lines. From his contemplation of the life to come, he glances momentarily aside to examine his
present position. 'I am old & ill': he quotes directly from 'The Man
and the Echo'. 'My flesh is heavy it weighs upon my heart but I
shall soon cast it off' expresses an idea found also in the first draft
of 'Sailing to Byzantium': 'For many loves have I taken off my
clothes . . . but now I will take off my body.' The simile 'as light as a
bird', far from being idle decoration, introduces an important
symbol that recurs frequently in Yeats's work. He commonly
depicts the souls of the dead as birds. In *Deirdre* the First Musician
makes his ominous prophecy of the lovers' union in death, 'Eagles
have gone into their cloudy bed.'[1]

On F. 2*v* the poet asserts his belief in the immanence of God in
all things, but at the same time refuses to yield allegiance to the
Christian Godhead.

III

> *God is in all things, ~~yet~~ but*
>
> *~~is~~ all is a way of putting*
>
> *"thinking masks" — ~~I will have (. .)~~*
>
> *I shut him out. I call to me Cuchulain*
>
> *~~from~~ years that seemed so new 30 yrs*
>
> *ago as I (. . . . .)*
>
> *(. . . . .)*

As in the last stanza of 'The Statues' he invokes, in the great shade
of Cuchulain, a proudly pagan ideal of man's heroic self-reliance.

[1] *Collected Plays of W. B. Yeats*, 1953, p. 202.

On F. 3r he makes the contrast more explicit in his redrafting of
section III.

III

God comes to us in all things—in our

passing thoughts in the sun in the leaves

he is in all this morning & (.   ) Yet I
      I would   could
would not ask him for anything & I will

be satisfied by death did I not know

that it he who asks who refuses to ask.

But I throw from my heart all images of

submission—I have found the great

Cuchullain in my arrogant heart. There

is nothing that I have not will willed

The second prose draft opens on F. 3v with recapitulation, but
section II introduces a new variation on the theme of death's un-
importance.

I

First principles

"Eternity to Eternity' etc

The common people and their women

II

Death nothing—if the sky falls &

falling bombs—children hands & dance—

The soul out lives all things &

makes itself today as it pleases

III

Let the bombs fall—let them destroy the

hateful cities— ~~(.)~~

The talk of falling bombs recalls the opening of 'Lapis Lazuli', a poem written in 1936 but first published in March 1938:

> if nothing drastic is done
> Aeroplane and Zeppelin will come out,
> Pitch like King Billy bomb-balls in
> Until the town lie beaten flat.

The vision of physical disorder caused by falling bombs he contrasts with an image of children dancing. As in 'The Double Vision of Michael Robartes' and 'Long-legged Fly', Yeats uses a child's dance as a symbol of bodily and spiritual harmony. 'The soul out lives all things'—even the falling bombs. Indeed, in an outburst of rage against 'the hateful cities' of the materialistic age he so despised, like a vengeful prophet he bids the bombs fall.

The third prose draft begins on F. 4*r*. Though structurally it has much in common with F. 1*r*, the differences are significant.

I

I believe as did the old sages

who sat under the palm trees

the banyan trees, or among

those snow bound rocks, ~~and~~

a thousand years before ~~Chri~~ *Christ*

was born; I believe as did the

monks of the Mareotic sea,

as do ~~every n~~ *country men*

who see the old fighting men

& their fine women coming out

of the mountain, moving from

mountain to mountain

II

And this is what I believe that

~~*man*~~ *man stands between two*

The 'old saints' are now—more sensibly—'the old sages'; 'saint' having predominantly Christian overtones. That some sit under banyan trees identifies them as Buddhists: though Gautama Buddha, in fact, lived in the sixth century B.C. The Sidhe, or spirit population of Irish folklore, are more clearly delineated in this draft. 'The old fighting men & their fine women . . . moving from mountain to mountain' appear in the haunting refrain to 'Three Songs to One Burden': 'From mountain to mountain ride the fierce horsemen.' An early version of the first song is to be found on F. 13*v*.

F. 5*r* follows on directly from F. 4*r*.

eternities, that of ~~*this family*~~*, his*

race that of his soul. Further

I declare that man serves there

sword in hand ~~*or with armed*~~

~~*mind*~~ *& with an armoured mind That*

a ~~*race is born*~~ *only so armed does*

man pick the right mate, & only

~~*when*~~ *only in the midst in the midst*

of a conflict, not straining all his

mind & his body & to the utmost

has he wisdom enough to choose

his right mate. The wisdom I

seek is written on a sword, mirrored

on a sword ~~who wrapped in a pie~~

on Sato's sword, a sword wrapped

Yeats's train of thought here enters the philosophical jungle of *A Vision*. Briefly, he believed with Blake that: 'Without Contraries there is no Progression. Attraction and Repulsion, Reason and Energy, Love and Hate are necessary to Human Existence.'[1] Happiness, wisdom, and perfection are attained only by preserving the tension between these opposites. Richard Ellmann tells how Yeats upset the Indian Professor Bose, who came to see him in 1937, when he replied to Bose's request for a message to India: 'Let 100,000 men of one side meet the other. That is my message to India.' He then, as Bose described the scene, 'strode swiftly across the room, took up Sato's sword, and unsheathed it dramatically and shouted, "Conflict, more conflict!"'.[2] Of Sato's sword, given to Yeats as a present, we hear in 'A Dialogue of Self and Soul':

> *My Self.*   Montashigi, third of his family, fashioned it
> Five hundred years ago, about it lie
> Flowers from I know not what embroidery—
> Heart's purple—and all these I set
> For emblems of the day against the tower
> Emblematical of the night,
> And claim as by a soldier's right
> A charter to commit the crime once more.

In section III on F. 6*r* God is not mentioned as on F. 2*v* and F. 3*r*: attention instead is concentrated on the soul.

in a woman's old embroidery.

III

I declare that no evil

can happen to the soul except

[1] 'The Marriage of Heaven and Hell', *The Complete Writings of William Blake*, edited by Geoffrey Keynes, 1966, p. 149.
[2] Richard Ellmann, *The Identity of Yeats*, p. 8.

from the soul—that death
   a brief   brief
is parting & ~~a passing sickness~~

What matter though the skies

drop for—children take hands

& dance

At this point it would seem that Yeats turned back to F. 5*v* and considered not the living but the dead, who (as described in Book IV of *A Vision*) 'recreate their old lives'.

                          writhe in remorse
I think the dead suffer remorse

for as I have described &·

re create their old lives for

as I have described. There are

modern popular plays upon the

subject & much in the folk lore

of all countries. In it they

play & sport suffer remorse

because of its share while (.) living

humans in the destruction of the

ancient houses. That destruction

is taking place all over Ireland

today. In a few cases the

cause has been very much what

I have described but in more

cases (.) for power or because the

> [1] *new Governments have lost interest. I know that*
>
> [1] *when old family* ~~*pictu have been sold*~~
>
> [1] *silver, pictures furniture have been sold*

Yeats cancelled all but the last three lines with a diagonal stroke of his pen. The dead he is concerned with here suffer remorse for their part in the betrayal of Ireland's heroic heritage to what in 'In the Seven Woods' he calls the 'new commonness . . . crying about the streets'. This for him is typified by 'the destruction of the ancient houses', a theme to which he often returns—notably in his poems about Coole.

2

This ends the prose drafts and on F. 7r rhyme enters the poem with the early version of the final epitaph already mentioned: 'Cast a cold eye' is a marked improvement on 'Turn that indifferent eye'.

> *Draw rain. Draw breath.*
>   *Cast a cold*
> ~~*Turn that indifferent*~~ *eye*
>
> *On life, on death.*
>
> *Horse man pass by*
>
>
> *Drop bombs & blow the pavement etc*
>
>
> *What the great forefathers did*
>   *Measurement began our*
> ~~*Here the origin of our*~~ *might*
> *Forms a stark Egyptian thought*
>   *(.   )*
> ~~*Forms a (.   ) Phideas wrought*~~
> *That this purpose had been set*
>
> *Let children should an airplane*
>   ~~*Bomb the Drop bombs, & blow the city*~~ *etc*

⌒
·
·
·
⌣ 2

[1] Indicates a line inserted from the top of the page.
[2] Having reached the foot of this page, Yeats turned it on its side and wrote five words along the right-hand edge.

~~Bombs upon the city rain~~

Or the deafening cannon sound

Catch hands & dance in round
                              that
explosion on ~~*their*~~ (.   ) *rain*

Bombs upon this (.   )

Or

A new and important theme emerges from this page. With 'Here
the origin of our might', corrected to 'Measurement began our
might', Yeats introduces a theme central also to 'The Statues' and
elaborated in *On the Boiler*:

There are moments when I am certain that art must once again accept
those Greek proportions which carry into plastic art the Pythagorean
numbers, those faces which are divine because all there is empty and
measured.[1]

The subsequent jottings show him toying with the curious image—
found first on F. 3*v* and later to be abandoned—of children dancing
in a symbolic circle while 'cannon sound' and bombs fall. This idea
he continues and expands on F. 8*r*:

Before he can accomplish fate

He recovers all his mind
                              stand
       For an instant ~~*is*~~ *at ease*
Or
       Laughs aloud as though·in peace.

Let children should an airplane

~~*Children that is an airplane*~~
       Some neighbouring city pavement stain
~~*Bombs upon the city rain.*~~
                              Or the deadly cannon sound
~~*That is the cannon's deafening sound*~~

~~*Hand in hand dance in a round.*~~

[1] *On the Boiler*, p. 37.

> *Catch their hands & dance in a round*
>
> *That passing moment makes it sweet*
>
> *When male & female organ meet*
>
> ~~*When*~~ *or enemy looks on enemy*
>
> *Timeless man's this honey bee*

Now it is not only children who discover peace at the centre of conflict, but also lovers and soldiers. The sexual act was, of course, closely associated in Yeats's mind with the perpetual motion of the interpenetrating gyres described in *A Vision*.

3

Ff. 9*r* to 13*r* constitute the third phase of the poem's composition: the first complete, but rough, verse draft. I have a strong suspicion that it was preceded by other, incomplete fragments of rough verse draft, but having found no trace of these I move now to F. 9*r*.

> ~~*His*~~
>
> ~~*Creed Convictions*~~
>
> *Under Ben Bulben*

I

>   *sages*
> *Swear by what the* ~~*sages*~~ *spoke*
>
> *Round the Mareotic Lake,*
>
> *That the Witch of Atlas knew;*
>   *Spoke and set all the*
> ~~*Swear before a*~~ *cock* ~~*can*~~ *crow.*
>   *by*   *swear by horsemen, swear by women*
> *By those horsemen or those women*
>
> *Complexions lift above the human,*
>
> ~~*All those faces that appear in*~~
>
> ~~*Tuatha de Dananan of Erin,*~~

That
~~*Pale*~~ *long visaged company*

That airs an immortality
                 in
Completeness ~~of~~ their passions won.

Now they ride the wintry dawn

Where Ben bulben sets the scene;

Here's the gist of ~~th~~ what they mean.

II

Many times man lives & dies,

Between his two eternities

That of race & that of soul;
and   Ireland
Ancient ~~Erin~~ knew it all.

Whether ~~a~~ man die in his bed

This draft shows the evolution of the poem's title from 'Creed' to 'His Convictions' and, finally, the impersonal 'Under Ben Bulben'. A similar movement from the subjective to the objective is visible in the first line, where the statement 'I believe . . .' has given place to the terse imperative 'Swear . . .'. Shelley's Witch of Atlas, who here makes her first appearance, knows—as 'the sages spoke'—of the immortality of the soul:

> She, all those human figures breathing there
>   Beheld as living spirits—to her eyes
> The naked beauty of the soul lay bare,
>   And often through a rude and worn disguise
> She saw the inner form most bright and fair . . .   (Stanza LXVI)

The opening of 'Under Ben Bulben' would seem to have its roots in Yeats's researches of almost forty years before. His essay, dated 1900, on 'The Philosophy of Shelley's Poetry' contains many references to the Witch of Atlas, as, for example: 'When the Witch has passed in her boat from the caverned river, that is doubtless her own destiny, she passes along the Nile "by Moeris and the Mareotic lakes . . .".' At the essay's eloquent end he speaks of 'that far household where the undying gods await all whose souls have become simple as flame, whose bodies have become quiet as an agate lamp'.[1]

The opening sentence of the finished poem has puzzled many people, since it sounds as if the Witch of Atlas 'Spoke and set the cocks a-crow'. No cocks crow in Shelley's poem. This draft shows that Yeats wrote at first 'Swear before a cock can crow'. In changing it to 'Spoke and set all the cock crow', he intended, I believe, the sages rather than the Witch to be the subject of 'Spoke'. The cock as a symbol of resurrection appears in 'Two Kings', 'Solomon and the Witch', and 'Byzantium', and is conceivably related to the cock that crowed over S. Peter.

The 'old fighting men' of F. 4r here become, significantly, 'horsemen': the horse for Yeats was a symbol of spirited and courageous nobility, and time and again in his poems he refers to the good horsemanship of those whom he admires—such as Robert Gregory, Con Markiewicz, and George Pollexfen. In a note to 'The Hosting of the Sidhe' he explains the 'long visaged company':

The gods of ancient Ireland, the Tuatha de Danaan, or the tribes of the goddess Danu, or the Sidhe, from Aes Sidhe, or Sluagh Sidhe, the people of the Faery Hills, as these words are usually explained, still ride the country as of old. Sidhe is also Gaelic for wind, and certainly the Sidhe have much to do with the wind.[2]

Section II of the poem is continued on F. 10r.

> rifle ~~shoot~~ knock
> Or the ~~cannon strike~~ him dead,
>
> A brief parting from those dear
>
> Is the worst man has to fear.
>   Those   toil be
> Though ~~Though~~ grave diggers ~~work is~~ long
>   ~~his~~ their   their
> Sharp ~~is~~ spade s, ~~his~~ muscle strong

---

[1] *Essays and Introductions*, 1961, pp. 85 and 95.

[2] Peter Allt and Russell K. Alspach, eds., *The Variorum Edition of the Poems of W. B. Yeats*, 1957, p. 802.

can   lay   ~~their~~
~~have~~ they ~~laid~~   *Where* ~~can he lay his~~ *buried men?*
      their

Back in the human mind again.

III

                      ~~knew heard~~
          ~~You that heard John Mitchell prayed heard John Mitchel~~
                                                              ~~pray~~
                  ~~might~~   ~~in his day~~
          ~~That God might send war in his day before he died:~~

[1] *You that Mitchell's prayer have heard*

[1] *'Send war in our time O Lord',*

Know that when all words are said

And a man is fighting mad,

Something drops from eyes long blind,

He recovers his whole mind,

For an instant stands at ease,
                    ~~and~~ *his heart's*
Laughs aloud ~~and seems~~ *at peace.*

Even the wisest man grows tense

With some sort of violence

Before he can accomplish fate

Know his work or choose his mate

~~So what's the odds if war must come~~

~~From Moscow, from Berlin, or Rome.~~

~~From London, Moscow, Berlin, Rome.~~
        So
~~Let children should an aeroplane~~

~~Some neighbouring city pavement stain,~~

~~Or Should the deafening cannon sound~~

[1] Indicates a line inserted, at the pointing of an arrow, from the top of the page.

The 'cannon' that gave Yeats so much trouble on Ff. 7*r* and 8*r* is superseded by the more modern and appropriate 'rifle'. The grave-diggers must surely be related to those in *Hamlet*, a play that we know to have been in his mind at this time as the Prince is twice mentioned in the poem 'Lapis Lazuli'. The image of them burying their dead in the *anima mundi* appears also in *On the Boiler* which Yeats was writing at about this time:

No educated man to-day accepts the objective matter and space of popular science, and yet deductions made by those who believed in both dominate the world . . . [and] . . . compel denial of the immortality of the soul by hiding from the mass of the people that the grave diggers have no place to bury us but in the human mind.[1]

The same train of thought that led Yeats to entitle this poem 'Creed' and begin it 'I believe' prompts him to introduce section II with John Mitchel's terrible parody of the sentence from the Order for Evening Prayer: 'Give us peace in our time, O Lord.' Mitchel[2] wrote in his *Jail Journal*: 'Give us war in our time, O Lord.'[3] Yeats, of course, takes this plea for conflict out of its nationalistic context and uses it to support his philosophic doctrine. At the foot of this page he crosses out his reference to an impending international conflict, perhaps lest this distract attention from the dominant philosophic meaning.

F. 11*r* follows on directly from F. 10*r*:

> *Clasp*
> ~~Lay hand in hand and~~
> ~~and~~
> ~~Clasp their hands & dance a ro in a round.~~
> *or*
> *The passing moment makes it sweet*
>
> *When male & female organ meet*
> *at*
> *Or enemy looks ~~on~~ enemy,*
>
> *Timeless man's this honey bee.*

[1] p. 26.

[2] 1815–75: he founded *United Irishmen*, was tried for sedition and transported, but returned to Ireland and became an M.P.

[3] *Jail Journal, or Five Years in British Prisons*, 1856, p. 315.

~~III~~ IV

Poet ~~s~~ & sculptor ~~s~~ do the work,
          the
Nor let ~~the~~ modish painter ~~s~~ shirk
          his   ~~their~~
What ~~his~~ great forefathers did,

Bring the soul of man to God

Make him fill the cradles right.

Measurement began our might.

Forms a stark Egyptian thought,

Forms that gentler Phideas wrought.

Michael Angelo left a proof

On the Sistine chapel roof
          but half awakened
Where his ~~homo-sexual~~ Adam

Can disturb globe-trotting madam

Till her bowels are in heat,
          ~~a~~
~~That this purpose had been set~~   Proof what purpose had been set

Before the secret working ~~min~~ mind :

Profane perfection of man kind.

Quatro cento put in paint

On backgrounds for a God or saint,

Here, for the first time, Yeats names the specific audience he has in
mind: 'Poet & sculptor do the work, Nor let the modish painter
shirk What his great forefathers did.' An artist is passing on the
tenets of his artistic creed to the artists who will follow him. Though
I use the word 'artist' in its widest sense, it should be remembered
that not only were Yeats's father and brother celebrated painters
but that he himself at one time went to art school. So now, tracing

M

the history of proportion in the visual arts from the ancient Egyptians to the Greeks to Michael Angelo, he returns to a theme already handled in 'Michael Robartes and the Dancer' and the last stanza of 'Long-legged Fly':

> That girls at puberty may find
> The first Adam in their thought,
> Shut the door of the Pope's chapel,
> Keep those children out.
> There on the scaffolding reclines
> Michael Angelo.

In short, Yeats sees it as an artist's duty to provide true heroic and sexual images to kindle the imagination of generations to come. He it is who must 'Bring the soul of man to God, Make him fill the cradles right'. The curious image of the cradles is also found in the drafts—though not the final version—of 'In Memory of Eva Gore-Booth and Con Markiewicz' as:

> For widow Nature still
> Has those cradles left to fill.[1]

On F. 12*r* Yeats outlines the history of art, as applicable to his 'system', from the Quattrocento painters to those of the English Romantic period.

> *Gardens where a soul's at ease;*
>
> *The soul's perfection is from peace;*
>
> *Where everything that meets the eye,*
>
> *Flowers & grass & cloudless sky*
>
> *Resembles forms that are or seem*
>
> *When sleepers wake & yet still dream*
>
> *And when it's vanished still declare*
>
> *~~That~~ with only bed & bed stead there*
>
> *That heaven had opened.*

---

[1] See Jon Stallworthy, *Between the Lines*, p. 171.

run

Gyres ~~ran~~ on :

When that greater dream

~~And all man's holiest thought~~ had gone,

and

Calvert & Palmer, Wilson, Claude

Prepared

~~Made~~ a rest for the people of God

Palmer's phrase but after that

Confusion fell upon our thought

V

Irish poets learn your trade,

Sing whatever is well made,

Scorn the sort now growing up,

All out of shape from toe to ‡ top

Their unremembering hearts & heads

Base born products of base beds,

Sing the peasantry & then

hardriding country gentlemen,

It is interesting to see him change the line: 'And all man's holiest thought had gone', to 'When that greater dream had gone'. I suspect he was loath to suggest that medieval Christianity had a monopoly of 'man's holiest thought'. Yeats almost certainly came to be acquainted with the work of Calvert and Palmer while preparing his 1893 edition of *The Poems of William Blake*. At one time we know he considered writing a book on Calvert. Raymond Lister writes that

Calvert's engravings, and to a lesser extent his pictures, depict a symbolic world, a place of dreamy peacefulness. . . . It is a world perceived by Yeats, who, apropos of Blake's wood-engravings for Thornton's *Virgil* wrote:

'. . . always in his [Blake's] boys and girls walking or dancing on smooth grass and in golden light, as in pastoral scenes cut upon wood or copper by his disciples Palmer and Calvert, one notices the peaceful Sweden-borgian heaven.'[1]

A heaven indeed, but hardly a Christian one. Calvert, like Yeats, could never bring himself to accept Christianity in its entirety.[2]

> Calvert & Palmer, Wilson and Claude
> Prepared a rest for the people of God
> Palmer's phrase

As with the prayer ascribed to John Mitchel at the start of section III, Yeats does not quote 'Palmer's phrase' exactly. In fact Palmer had said that Blake's work shows us: 'the drawing aside of the fleshly curtain and the glimpse which all the most holy, studious saints and sages[3] have enjoyed of that rest which remaineth to the people of God.'[4] Yeats had quoted this passage in 1896 in his essay entitled 'William Blake and his Illustrations to the *Divine Comedy*'.[5]

Whereas sections I and III of 'Under Ben Bulben' open with a general audience directly addressed ('Swear by what the sages spoke' and 'You that Mitchel's prayer have heard'), section IV is more specific ('Poet and sculptor, do the work,'); and section V more specific still ('Irish poets, learn your trade,'). As might have been expected, his last message is for the poets: let them preserve order, proportion, and good craftsmanship. His own language changes subtly here; becomes less colloquial, more measured and literary. This is typified by the rhetorical repetition of the impera-tive 'Sing'—a bardic, classical usage as in Virgil's *Arma virumque cano*. The 'last romantic' bids his successors praise peasant and country gentleman, monk, drunkard, and aristocrat; figures beyond the perimeter of unromantic, bourgeois society.

F. 13*r* concludes the complete verse draft.

> *The holiness of monks & after*
>
> *Porter drinkers randy laughter;*

[1] *Explorations*, 1962, p. 44.

[2] 'W. B. Yeats and Edward Calvert', *The Irish Book*, ii. 3/4; 1963, p. 75.

[3] Compare Yeats's interchange of these nouns in his drafts of the first line of 'Under Ben Bulben', pp. 150 and 154.

[4] A. H. Palmer, *Life and Letters of Samuel Palmer*, 1892, p. 16. The phrase, in fact, is first found in St. Paul's Epistle to the Hebrews 4: 9: 'There remaineth therefore a rest to the people of God.'

[5] *Essays and Introductions*, 1961, p. 125.

Sing the lords and ladies gay

That were beaten into the clay

Through seven heroic centuries;
      Cast your mind
~~*Set your thought*~~ *on other days*

That we in coming days may be

Still the indomitable ~~Irishry~~ Irishry.

VI

      bare
Under Benbulben's ~~Western~~ head
In Drum cliff Churchyard Yeats is laid
      ancestor
An ~~cestor~~ was rector there

Long years ago, a church stands near
            side
By the road an ancient cross.
            ~~*to lie about our loss*~~ *braggs ~~of the country's~~ loss*
No marble ~~lies public man, lies lie about man's~~ loss,
                  the braggs of ~~the country's~~ loss

On limestone quarried near ~~that~~ spot Ireland's newest loss

By his command these words are cut

      Cast a cold eye

      On life, on death;

      Horse man pass by.

W B Y

Sept 4

1938

The lines 'Sing the lords and ladies gay That were beaten into the clay' suggest the influence—no doubt subconscious—of Frank O'Connor's translation 'Kilcash': 'The earls, the lady, the people

Beaten into the clay.'[1] Yeats had earlier echoed O'Connor's translation in 'The Curse of Cromwell' ('The lovers and the dancers are
beaten into the clay'), a poem that he published in his Cuala *Broadsides* in August 1937, three months after 'Kilcash' had appeared in
the same series. O'Connor has written that the translation 'was one
of [Yeats's] favourite poems, and there is a good bit of his work in
it'.[2] We see from this page that section VI gave him trouble. Ben
Bulben, whose back he so often climbed 'in boyhood . . . with rod
and fly, Or the humbler worm', had set the scene at the start of the
poem; and to this mountain at life's end and poem's end he returns.
The cyclic movement that dominated his later thought brings him
to cross and churchyard where his great-grandfather, the Reverend
John Yeats, was rector:

> He that in Sligo at Drumcliff
> Set up the old stone Cross,
> That red-headed rector in County Down,
> A good man on a horse.

While Lister is correct in saying that Yeats 'could never bring himself to accept Christianity in its entirety',[3] 'Under Ben Bulben'
shows how deeply Christian history and images had interpenetrated
his thought. In the last analysis, however, he has the courage of his
pagan convictions. His epitaph is addressed to a horseman who may
be one of the Sidhe, or one of the 'Hard-riding country gentlemen';
either the living or the dead—or both.

> Cast a cold eye
> On life, on death;
> Horse man pass by.

The line 'Draw rein, draw breath' has been dropped: why? Only
the living draw breath and Yeats's omission of these beautifully
balanced imperatives suggests that he had a spiritual horseman in
mind, or at any rate wanted to preserve the ambiguity.[4] Drumcliffe
churchyard may be seen as a symbolic crossroads, for there the

---

[1] *The Wild Bird's Nest: Poems from the Irish*, 1932, p. 24.

[2] Frank O'Connor, *Kings, Lords, & Commons*, 1959, p. 100.

[3] Loc. cit.

[4] My view that this omission is necessary and an improvement supersedes a contrary
opinion in *Between the Lines*, p. 6.

Sligo–Lissadell road that carries its 'hard-riding country gentlemen'
intersects at right angles the route of the 'fierce horsemen' who
ride 'from mountain to mountain', from Knocknarea to Ben
Bulben.[1]

This at first sight may seem a surprising epitaph for a poet who
could elsewhere

> pray—for fashion's word is out
> And prayer comes round again—
> That I may seem, though I die old,
> A foolish, passionate man.

The paradox is stated more explicitly in the closing lines of 'The
Fisherman', where the poet imagined

> A man who does not exist,
> A man who is but a dream;
> And cried, 'Before I am old
> I shall have written him one
> Poem maybe as cold
> And passionate as the dawn.'

In his drafts of 'The Statues' he had written of 'cold marble forms'
and 'doric marble cold as moon or star',[2] but (in the words of the
finished poem)

> boys and girls, pale from the imagined love
> Of solitary beds, knew what they were,
> That passion could bring character enough . . .

Great statues, great paintings—all time-resisting works of art—are
in their technical perfection 'cold', but at the same time products
of an artist's passionate integrity. By 'Cast a cold eye' Yeats means
on one level (of many) in this context, I believe, not so much a
passionless as an artist's discerning eye; one—like his own—fixed
equally on the natural and supernatural, 'On life, on death'. The
ghostly horsemen of the Sidhe are said in section I of the poem to
have won 'completeness of their passions' and this, Yeats was convinced, only the dead could do. To win completeness of one's
passions, however, is not to reject them. Again, if he was addressing

---

[1] I am indebted to Dr. Oliver Edwards for this suggestion.
[2] See pp. 125 and 129.

a phantom, its eye might well be described as cold. The previous
year he had written:

The heroes of Shakespeare convey to us through their looks, or through
the metaphorical patterns of their speech, the sudden enlargement of
their vision, their ecstasy at the approach of death: 'She should have
died hereafter,' 'Of many thousand kisses, the poor last,' 'Absent thee
from felicity awhile.' They have become God or Mother Goddess, the
pelican, 'My baby at my breast,' but all must be cold; no actress has ever
sobbed when she played Cleopatra, even the shallow brain of a producer
has never thought of such a thing. The supernatural is present, cold
winds blow across our hands, upon our faces, the thermometer falls,
and because of that cold we are hated by journalists and groundlings.[1]

The lines immediately preceding the epitaph, which we can see
Yeats struggling over on F. 13r, he recasts on F. 12v:

A century ago, a church stands near

By the roadside an ancient cross.

No marble, no conventional phrase

On limestone quarried near the spot

By his command etc

The first line here moves one stage further from its final form of
'Long years ago, a church stands near': while the third line reaches
its final form. 'No marble, no conventional phrase' is much more
appropriate than 'No marble brags of Ireland's loss', which has
more than a hint of a forced rhyme.

It will by now be clear that the fourth phase of the poem's composition—the typescript stage—saw fewer changes than any other.
Of the three typescripts, each of three pages, I consider only that
which from its alterations I deduce to be the last. I therefore pass
over Ff. 14r to 19r and come to F. 20r, on which the following lines
differ from the previous manuscript drafts.

Line 4.   Spoke and set all the cock crow.
                 becomes
                 Spoke and set all the cocks a-crow.

[1] *Essays and Introductions*, p. 523.

Lines 5-9.   Swear by horseman, swear by women,
               Complexions lift above the human,
               That long visaged company
               That airs an immortality
               Completeness in their passions won.
               become
               Swear by those horsemen, by those women,
               Complexion and form prove superhuman,
               That pale, long visaged company
               That airs an immortality
               Completeness of their passions won;

Line 18.   . . . rifle knock . . .   *becomes*   . . . rifle knocks . . .

Line 21.   . . . toil be long   *becomes*   . . . toil is long

Line 23—originally a rhetorical question—

               Where can they lay their buried men?
               becomes
               They but thrust their buried men

Line 30.   He recovers his whole mind,
           becomes
           He completes his partial mind,

F. *21r*: Line 45.   Michael Angelo . . . *becomes*   Michaelangelo . . .

Line 50.   Proof what purpose had been set
           becomes
           Proof that there's a purpose set

Line 64.   Calvert & Palmer, Wilson, and Claude
           becomes
           Calvert and Wilson, Blake and Claude

F. *22r*: Line 84.   . . . Benbulben's head
           becomes
           . . . Ben Bulben's head

Line 87.   A century ago, . . .   *becomes*   Long years ago; . . .

Line 88.   By the roadside . . . *becomes* By the road . . .

This typescript is undated, but on an earlier one Yeats has set below his initials: 'Correct. Sept 23'.

The version of 'Under Ben Bulben' that Yeats, on his last night in Dublin, read to Higgins would presumably be that of the final typescript. The alterations that Mrs. Yeats received from her husband on the day before he died might have been that to line 4, whereby '. . . set all the cocks a-crow' became '. . . set the cocks a-crow'; and that to line 8, whereby '. . . airs an immortality' became '. . . air in immortality'. The only other changes between typescript and final text are minor improvements of spelling and punctuation, which were probably made by Mrs. Yeats or a publisher rather than by Yeats himself.

'Under Ben Bulben' is a fitting conclusion to the life and work of a poet whose lifelong concern was to 'hammer [his] thoughts into unity'. It brings full circle the poetic career of one for whom the circle was a dominant symbol. The themes and interests of his early manhood—Irish folklore and history, the occult, Shelley, Blake, and the English Romantic painters of the late nineteenth century— fit like tesserae into the mosaic pattern of his later 'system'. As Michael Angelo, though dead, continues to influence the living with heroic images 'On the Sistine Chapel roof', so Yeats still speaks from 'Under Ben Bulben'.

SELECT BIBLIOGRAPHY

WORKS BY W. B. YEATS

Autobiographies, Macmillan, 1955.
A Vision, T. Werner Laurie, 1925; second edition, Macmillan, 1937.
Essays and Introductions, Macmillan, 1961.
Explorations, Macmillan, 1962.
Mythologies, Macmillan, 1959.
On The Boiler, Cuala Press, 1939.
ALLT, P., and ALSPACH, R. K., eds., *The Variorum Edition of the Poems of W. B. Yeats*, Macmillan, 1957.
ALSPACH, R. K., ed., *The Variorum Edition of the Plays of W. B. Yeats*, Macmillan, 1966.
WADE, A., ed., *The Letters of W. B. Yeats*, Rupert Hart-Davis, 1954.
WELLESLEY, D., ed., *Letters on Poetry from W. B. Yeats to Dorothy Wellesley*, Oxford Univ. Press, reissued with an Introduction by Kathleen Raine, 1964.

Books Relevant to the Study of Last Poems and Plays

BRADFORD, CURTIS, *Yeats at Work*, Southern Illinois Univ. Press, 1965.
ELLMANN, RICHARD, *The Identity of Yeats*, second edition, Macmillan, 1964.
—— *Yeats/The Man and the Masks*, Macmillan, 1949.
ENGELBERG, EDWARD, *The Vast Design/Patterns in W. B. Yeats's Aesthetic*, Univ. of Toronto Press, 1964.
HENN, T. R., *The Lonely Tower*, second edition, Methuen, 1965.
HONE, JOSEPH, *W. B. Yeats 1865-1939*, second edition, Macmillan, 1962.
JEFFARES, A. N., *W. B. Yeats/Man and Poet*, reissued with corrections, Routledge, 1962.
—— and CROSS, K. G. W., eds., *In Excited Reverie/A Centenary Tribute*, Macmillan, 1965.
KIRBY, SHEELAH, *The Yeats Country*, Dolmen Press, 1962.
KOCH, VIVIENNE, *W. B. Yeats/The Tragic Phase/A Study of the Last Poems*, Routledge, 1951.
PARKINSON, THOMAS, *W. B. Yeats/The Later Poetry*, Univ. of California Press, 1964.
RAJAN, B., *W. B. Yeats/a critical introduction*, Hutchinson, 1965.
SAUL, GEORGE BRANDON, *Prolegomena to the Study of Yeats's Poems*, Univ. of Pennsylvania Press, 1957.
STALLWORTHY, JON, *Between the Lines/W. B. Yeats's Poetry in the Making*, second impression with corrections, Clarendon Press, 1965.

—— *Yeats: Last Poems / Casebook Series*, Macmillan, 1968.

STOCK, A. G., *W. B. Yeats: His Poetry and Thought*, Cambridge Univ. Press, 1961.

TORCHIANA, DONALD, *W. B. Yeats and Georgian Ireland*, Northwestern Univ. Press, 1966.

UNTERECKER, JOHN, *A Reader's Guide to W. B. Yeats*, Thames and Hudson, 1959.

URE, PETER, *Yeats the Playwright / A Commentary on Character and Design in the Major Plays*, Routledge, 1963.

WILSON, F. A. C., *W. B. Yeats and Tradition*, Gollancz, 1958.

—— *Yeats's Iconography*, Gollancz, 1960.

Articles Relevant to the Study of Last Poems and Plays

ALLEN, JAMES L., 'Yeats's "Long-legged Fly"', *Explicator*, xxi (1963), item 51.

BOGAN, LOUISE, 'William Butler Yeats', *The Atlantic Monthly*, clxi, 5 (1938), pp. 637-44.

DISKIN, PATRICK, 'A Source for Yeats's "The Black Tower"', *Notes and Queries*, viii. 3 (1961), pp. 107-8.

DYSON, A. E., 'An Analysis of Yeats's "Long-legged Fly"', *The Critical Survey*, ii. 2 (1965), pp. 101-3.

GARAB, ARRA M., 'Fabulous Artifice: Yeats's "Three Bushes" Sequence', *Criticism*, vii. 3 (1965), pp. 235-49.

—— 'Yeats and *The Forged Casement Diaries*', *English Language Notes*, ii (1965), pp. 289-92.

JEFFARES, A. N., '"Gyres" in the Poetry of W. B. Yeats', *English Studies*, xxvii (1946), pp. 65-74.

—— 'Yeats's "The Gyres": Sources and Symbolism', *Huntington Library Quarterly*, xv, pp. 89-97.

KEITH, W. J., 'Yeats's Arthurian Black Tower', *Modern Language Notes*, lxxv. 2 (1960), pp. 119-23.

LABISTOUR, MARION, 'Lapis Lazuli', *The Critical Survey*, iii. 1 (1966), pp. 13-16.

LEAVIS, F. R., 'The Great Yeats and the Latest', *Scrutiny*, viii. 4 (1940), pp. 437-40.

MENDEL, S., 'Yeats's "Lapis Lazuli"', *Explicator*, xix. 9 (1961), item 64.

PARTRIDGE, E. B., 'Yeats's "The Three Bushes"—Genesis and Structure', *Accent*, xvii. 2 (1957), pp. 67-80.

PERRINE, L., 'Yeats's "An Acre of Grass", *Explicator*, xxii. 8 (1964), item 64.

SICKELS, E. M., 'Yeats's "The Gyres", 6', *Explicator*, xv. 9 (1957), item 60.

SOUTHAM, B. C., 'Yeats's "Long-legged Fly"', *Explicator*, xxi (1963), item 51.

—— 'Yeats's "Long-legged Fly"', *Explicator*, xxii (1964).

URE, PETER, '"The Statues": A Note on the Meaning of Yeats's Poem', *Review of English Studies*, xv. 99 (1949), pp. 254-7.

INDEX

PRINTED IN GREAT BRITAIN
AT THE UNIVERSITY PRESS, OXFORD
BY VIVIAN RIDLER
PRINTER TO THE UNIVERSITY